Author's Note

After six years' service in the R.A.F. during the war, Bernard Benjamin completed his first degree, in English, and started teaching. He was subsequently Headmaster of four secondary schools in London, Essex and Cheshire. The last two schools were special schools for pupils with behaviour and learning handicaps. He was awarded an M.A. degree in Literature and a M.Ed. degree for research into the self-image of handicapped pupils.

In 1940 he married a ballet dancer, Beatrice Golka, and they raised a lively family of four sons and a daughter. He retired from teaching in 1985 and now spends his time, he says, learning.

D1102361

BENJAMIN'S
ELEMENTARY PRIMER
OF
ENGLISH GRAMMAR

Futura

A Futura Book

Copyright © Bernard Benjamin 1989

First published in Great Britain in 1989 by
Futura Publications, a Division of
Macdonald & Co (Publishers) Ltd
London & Sydney

ISBN 0 7088 4485 5

Printed in Great Britain at The Guernsey Press

Futura Publications
A Division of
Macdonald & Co (Publishers) Ltd
66–73 Shoe Lane
London EC4P 4AB

A member of Maxwell Pergamon Publishing
Corporation plc

For Beatrice
and my children
and grandchildren
and many thousands of others
who may remember the joyful battles

Contents

Introduction

Advocates for and against the teaching of formal English grammar in schools stand opposed almost equal in numbers. The weaponry of the arguments on both sides is probably equal in theory and sophistication and the open-endedness of the debate is unlikely to be resolved by any commission of inquiry or, indeed, any *diktat* from an enterprising Secretary of State for Education.

However, the antiformalists have for some decades had the edge and a feeling is growing that there is a balance here to be restored. Teachers of foreign languages in particular, observing the neglect of Latin and the virtual desertion of Greek, despair of the grammatical illiteracy of pupils beginning the study of a European language, where grammatical rules tend to demand a stricter response than in English. One senses a hardening of attitudes, leading to more grammatical awareness, away from the leniency of self-expression that has aimed to liberate pupils from bogeymen grammatists.

The difficulty is to know where to start. 'Nesfield' no longer lodges reassuringly in the locker desk, examinations no longer contain questions requiring grammatical knowledge for an answer, and the social, political and philosophical climate which ensured grammar a respectable niche in the curriculum has vanished. How, then, can we break this 'circle of unknowledge'? A good modern book of grammar might do it for us.*

The idea begs the question. Leave on one side the undefinable 'good'. A grammar book can be 'modern' in format, in presentation and in choice of examples etc., but grammar, as a subject to be taught, has two major in-built handicaps. The first is its all-embracing universality. No part can be omitted without doing damage to some other part; the interrelatedness of its many elements forms a seamless gown, not to be robbed of any of its threads. This precludes short-cuts, and ready-to-use, prepacked study-aids and requires sustained effort from pupils.

The second difficulty is the need to master tradition-al jargon in defining and describing grammatical practices. 'Apposition', 'predicative use', 'noun-equivalent' and terms such as these may be somewhat off-putting to today's schoolchildren, but they are unavoidable. No grammar primer should pretend that they can be replaced and ignored, no teacher of grammar can avoid the hard graft of familiarising his pupils with such terms.

The study of language, 'the last and deepest problem of the philosophic mind' (W.M. Urban, *Language and Reality*), is not a precise science, and teachers will not cease from quarrelling over defini-tions and conventions. This is to the good. Practition-ers in English teaching may quarrel openly with some of the nomenclature and usage suggested in this book, sure in the knowledge that a judicious show of disagreement will help their pupils' understanding of language as a living and vibrant activity.

Be it recognised, however, that in this primer the aim is to make the discipline of grammar as useful as possible to young scholars and to provide the practical basis of knowledge upon which many of them will build their individual pavilion of delight as they study further.

This Introduction was written before the publication (1989) of the National Curriculum where the study of grammar re-emerges as a prerequisite of English teaching.

First Definitions

Letters:	The twenty-six vowels and consonants of the alphabet.
Word:	A spoken or written unit of language.
Phrase:	A group of words expressing an idea, but usually without defining any action.
Clause:	A group of words with a finite verb, but leaving the full expression of an idea uncompleted.
Sentence:	A complete idea expressed in words, beginning with a capital letter and ending with a full stop.
Paragraph:	A number of sentences containing a general unity of theme.

Examples:

Letters:	Vowels: a, e, i, o, u and (sometimes) y. All other letters are consonants.
Word:	Can be very small, like 'me', 'if', 'so', or very long, like 'antidisestablishment-arianism'.
Phrase:	'a cup of tea' 'along the High Street' 'holding his bat in his hand' 'a quickly-moving, beautifully greeny-yellow songbird'.
Clause:	'When William reached the bus stop. . .' 'If the train comes in late. . .' '. . . that he ought to be at home'. '. . . which he wore like a soldier'.
Sentence:	'Go home!' 'The policeman took aim and fired.' 'Stop!' 'As the ship docked, men came forward to unload the cargo, which contained several bars of gold.'

The Eight Parts of Speech

Words are classified according to their **function** in a sentence, according to what they do. Identifying what words do in a sentence and how they relate to each other is called **parsing**.

Each word is a **part of speech**. There are eight parts of speech, and every word we use can be put into one of these categories.

Here are their names: Noun
Pronoun
Adjective
Verb
Adverb
Preposition
Conjunction
Interjection

Note: A part of speech can sometimes contain more than one word.

'**Mr Henry Smith**' is a man's name. It has three words,
  but is **one** part of speech.
'**Olympic Games**' is a world sporting event. It has two words,
  but is **one** part of speech.
'**Coca Cola**' is a drink. It has two words,
  but it is **one** part of speech.
'He **had been drinking** a cup of tea'. 'Had been drinking' describes the action of the man. It is three words,
  but is **one** part of speech.

Nouns

A **noun** is a word that identifies or names; it tells us what a thing or person is. There are thousands of naming-words, nouns, in the English language.

A noun can be the name of

> a person
> an object
> an action
> a place
> an idea
> a quality
> a feeling

What we need to know about **nouns**

1. What **kind** of noun is it?

2. What **gender** is it?

3. What **number**?

4. What **case** is it in?

These words, gender, number and case, are all grammatical terms which will be explained.

KINDS OF NOUNS

A **noun** will fit into one of four categories:

proper noun, common noun,
collective noun, abstract noun

A **proper noun** is a special name, the name of one particular person, one particular place, one special thing or event. E.g.

> John, Mary, Mr Frank Green, Mrs Sarah Brown (persons)
> London, Paris, Africa, Houses of Parliament (places)
> Maltesers, Austin Rover, Typhoo Tea, Concorde (things)
> Cup Final, Royal Wedding, Commonwealth Games (events).

Proper nouns always have capital letters and may, as will be seen above, consist of more than one word.

A **common noun** is the general, ordinary name of a person, thing, place or event. They are not special or particular; there will be many of them. Most nouns are common nouns. E.g.

> footballer, daughter, captain, driver (persons)
> book, planet, ship, knife, chair (things)
> country, town, river, field, city (places)
> cricket match, swimming gala, film show (events).

Common nouns never have a capital letter unless they begin a sentence, but they too can consist of more than one word. The following sentences show the difference between proper nouns and common nouns:

> **Ian Rush** (proper) is a good **footballer** (common)
> **Mars** (proper) is the red-looking **planet** (common)
> **Berlin** (proper) is a **town** (common) in a **country** (common) called **Germany** (proper)
> **'Mutiny on the Bounty'** (proper, **one** noun) was a very good **film** (common).

A **collective noun** is the name for a group of similar persons or things, where the group is regarded as one idea:

E.g. team, fleet, flock, herd, cluster, mob.

We talk about a 'team of cricketers', a 'fleet of ships', a 'flock of birds', a 'herd of cattle', a 'cluster of stars', a 'mob of gangsters'. The words 'team' 'fleet' 'flock' 'herd' 'cluster' and 'mob' represent a group of separate items – a collection. They are known as collective nouns.

Abstract nouns represent the qualities that persons or things have, actions they take, or conditions they find themselves in. These are names of qualities that persons or things possess but which cannot normally be seen, touched, heard or felt, but are understood in the mind. E.g.

wisdom (the quality of being wise)
truth   (the condition of not lying)
poverty (the state of being poor)
anger   (the emotion of being angry)
fighting (the action of being involved in a fight).

'Wisdom' cannot be seen, 'truth' cannot be touched, 'poverty' cannot be heard or 'anger' tasted. These words are names of ideas which are understood in our minds only and they are known as abstract nouns.

GENDER OF NOUNS

Gender in English has four categories, and these refer to the maleness or femaleness of the persons being named. Only very rarely does it describe a thing (we do sometimes refer to a 'ship' as 'she'), and inanimate objects have no personal gender in English. The four kinds of gender are:

masculine – denoting male persons or animals (m.)
feminine – denoting female persons or animals (f.)
common – denoting either male or female, not one in particular
neuter – having no sex definition at all.

Masculine (m.) and **feminine** (f.) are easily understood, e.g. for words such as workman (m.) girl (f.) actress (f.) bull (m.) prince (m.) husband (m.) peacock (m.) hostess (f.) widow (f.).

Common gender is used for words which can be of either sex, e.g. relation, person, worker, employer, friend, pupil, teacher, cub, puppy, baby, any of which can be either masculine or feminine.

Words without gender are described as **neuter**, e.g. car, house, city, book, cloud, tree, ball, school.

These words, and thousands like them, have no masculine/feminine qualities at all.

Note: Other languages, French and German for instance, regard words which we would consider neuter as either masculine or feminine; this makes gender a more important matter in their grammars.

NUMBER OF NOUNS

All nouns are either **singular** or **plural** in grammar. When a noun is the name of *one* thing, it is said to be **singular** (sing.). When it is the name of *more than one*, it is **plural** (pl.).

The normal rule for forming plurals is to add an 's' to the word, e.g.

one table, four table*s*,

one house, three house*s*

Some spelling rules have to be watched when forming plurals:

Some add 'es':	one glass, five glasses one bus, six buses.
'y' becomes 'ies':	one army, four armies one dolly, three dollies. Unless 'y' is preceded by a vowel, e.g. convoy, money, tray, valley.
'-o' words add 'es':	one potato, two potatoes. one hero, four heroes. (But watch some words, e.g. piano, pianos.)
'-fe' becomes '-ves':	one knife, three knives one shelf, two shelves. (But: one dwarf, two dwarfs one roof, three roofs.)

Some words change their forms in the plural:

one man, six men   one mouse, three mice
one child, four children one ox, seven oxen.

Some words have no singular:

scissors, news, gallows, tongs.

Summary of the noun so far

1. What kind is it?   proper
                           common
                           collective
                           abstract

2. What gender is it?   masculine
                           feminine
                           common
                           neuter

3. What number is it?   singular plural

Examples of parsing the noun

When we parse a word we explain its function in a
sentence. We state what part of speech it is and
how it relates grammatically to other words in that
sentence.

Consider this sentence:

The **messengers** of **King Richard** asked **John of
Gaunt** to occupy **Bedford** with a **platoon** of **sol-
diers**, but to see that no **harm** came to **Princess
Alice**, whose **beauty** he prized.

The nouns are printed in **bold** type. To parse them, we
have to say:

Noun	Kind	Gender	Number	
messengers	common	common (probably masculine)	plural	
King Richard	proper	masculine	singular	(two words)
John of Gaunt	proper	masculine	singular	(three words)
Bedford	proper	neuter	singular	

platoon	collective	neuter	singular	
soldiers	common	masculine	plural	
harm	abstract	neuter	singular	
Princess Alice	proper	feminine	singular	(two words)
beauty	abstract	neuter	singular	

Exercises

Put each noun set in italic type into the appropriate column: proper, common, collective or abstract.

A *group* of *nuns* could be seen walking down the *street*.

King Charles was supposed to be very proud.

He wanted *peace* more than anything else.

The *cast* of '*Julius Caesar*' was late for *rehearsal*.

The *school* of *fish* vanished without *warning*.

Channel Four has the best *ideas*.

I like '*Coronation Street*'; the *crowd* in it are great.

Not many think that *Parliament* gives us anything of great *value*.

There was much *criticism* of the *book*; it did not belong to the *selection* I chose.

Identify the **gender** of the nouns in this paragraph:

William swallowed the *cherry*, *stone* as well. It was his tenth, and *Cousin Sally* secretly thought he was a *pig*! Her *brother* winked at her and said, 'Can we have a *cherry*, too?'

William swallowed his twelfth. 'None left,' he said, '*Sally*'s eaten them all!'

'Oh, you *tale-teller*,' said Sally, '*Animals* wouldn't be so greedy. Even *puppies* share their *food* with each other.'

Her *cousin* stole out of the *room*, a big *shape* stuffed under his *jersey*. Both the *children* suspected that he had the *bowl* of *cherries* stuffed away.

Write six short sentences; three containing nouns in the **singular**, three with nouns in the **plural**.

Give the **kind, gender** and **number** of the nouns in italics.

Father gave his *daughter* a birthday present.
Macbeth is never able to sleep after Duncan's murder.
He bought a new *pack* of cards for the children.
The bull tossed *Lady Pompom* over the fence.
Tom was always asking his *uncles* for money.
Most people give money to *charity* at Christmas.
The farmer was proud of his prize *sows*.
Ideas never came quickly for Jimmy.
The *Caesars* were men of great power.
The cowboys drove their *herds* of wild cattle over the plains.

There are twenty other nouns in these sentences, not printed in italics. Pick them out, and give the **kind, gender** and **number** of those twenty.

THE FIRST STEPPING-STONE: NOUN TO PRONOUN

These two parts of speech are related like parent and child. As the example at the beginning of the next section shows, life for a noun without its pronoun substitute would be unsupportable and communication would be severely hampered if there were no pronouns to undertake their essential function of standing in the place of nouns.

It follows that just as we need to know the kind, gender and number of a noun, we need equally to understand the equivalent functions discharged by their corresponding pronouns.

Pronouns

As the word **pronoun** indicates, it takes the place of, or substitutes for, a **noun**.

Consider this passage:

> The **bus** drew away from the kerb. The **bus** turned a corner and found a car blocking the **bus's** way, so the **bus** backed into a side street where, unfortunately, the **bus** hit a car.

The five repetitions of the word 'bus' make the passage clumsy and strange. To avoid this, we can substitute for 'bus' a **pronoun**, a word to take its place, thus:

> The bus drew away from the kerb. **It** turned a corner and found a car blocking its way, so **it** backed into a side street where **it**, unfortunately, hit a car.

Pronouns are thus short words which take the place of all kinds of nouns.

What we need to know about **pronouns**

1. What **kind** of pronoun is it?
2. What **person** is it?
3. What **number** is it?
4. What **case** is it in?
5. What is its **function** in the sentence?

KINDS OF PRONOUNS

1. Personal
2. Demonstrative
3. Relative
4. Interrogative

PERSONAL PRONOUNS take the place of *persons* or *things*. In grammar, there are three **persons**: 1st, 2nd and 3rd.

1st person: 'I' (sing.)
'We' (plural)
These can be m. or f.

2nd person: 'You' sing. or plural, m. or f.
(Note: 'Thou' is the singular form of 'you', but it is no longer used except in biblical or dialect contexts.)

3rd person: Sing: 'He' (m.) and 'She' (f.) 'It' (neuter)
Plur: 'They' – all forms.

Personal pronouns change their form according to the **case** they are in. Although **cases** as a topic has not yet been discussed, it might be convenient to tabulate the forms here.

	1st per.	2nd per.	3rd per.			
Nominative case:	I	we	you	he	she	it	they
Accusative case:	me	us	you	him	her	it	them
Genitive case:	mine	ours	yours	his	hers	its	theirs

Examples of **pronouns** in sentences:

I gave **it** to **him**. ('I' – Jim Ford; 'it' – the watch; 'him' – Harry)
We asked **her** to keep **them** safe for **us**.
('We' – John and Mary; 'her' – Sally; 'them' – the jewels; 'us' – John and Mary)

If **it** is **theirs, you** ought not to give **it** to **him**.
('it' – the book; 'theirs' – Bill's and Anne's; 'you' –
Jack Spratt; 'him' – Vic Russel)

REFLEXIVE FORMS OF PERSONAL PRONOUNS

These 'reflect' the meaning back to the original
pronoun, and are formed by adding the suffix 'self'.
They are used for emphasis.

	Sing.	Plural
1st person:	myself	ourselves
2nd person:	yourself	yourselves
3rd person:	himself	
	herself	themselves
	itself	

DEMONSTRATIVE PRONOUNS take the place of
nouns and point out which one, or ones, are meant:

'This' and 'that' are used in the singular.
'These' and 'those' in the plural.

Examples:
This is what I bought. (this shirt . . .)
Give me **that**, please. (that pen . . .)
I saw **these** in the shop. (these socks . . .)
Those will do nicely. (those grapes . . .)

Note 1: As these words are also used as **adjectives**, it
is important to check their *function* in the sentence, e.g.

> **This** book is interesting. ('This' is an **adjective**,
> qualifying 'book')
> **This** is an interesting book. ('This' is a **pronoun**,
> taking the place of 'book')

Note 2: Demonstrative pronouns sometimes substitute for a whole phrase or sentence, not just a word, e.g.

This is how you do it (= a description of a method of doing something. The original might have been: '*By putting a screw in here* is how you do it'. The words in italics have been replaced by 'this').

I don't think he meant **that** (= 'I don't think he meant *you should come in late tonight*').

One and none

In the sentence '**One** of these men is a traitor', 'one' stands for 'one man', and is considered a demonstrative pronoun.

Similarly, in 'I want **none** of them to come with me', 'none' (not one) is a substitute for the noun idea, not one of 'those people'.

Note 1: 'None' is normally regarded as singular, e.g. '**None was** present at the meeting', but occasionally it can be used in a plural sense: 'Of the eighteen girls left in the final of the beauty competition, **none have** yet been rejected for the title' is a feasible sentence.

Note 2: 'One' can be used in the plural, 'ones', e.g. 'Of the two football teams, seventeen men were exhausted, but the five lazy **ones** were scarcely out of breath.'

'One', 'ones' and 'none' are all **demonstrative pronouns.**

RELATIVE PRONOUNS have two functions:

1. They substitute for a noun and
2. They join two ideas (clauses) together.

Consider:

> The train stopped at the signal.
> The signal was red.

These two sentences can be combined thus:

> The train stopped at the signal, **which** was red.

'Which' stands for 'signal'. It also joins together the two statements. It is a **relative pronoun**.

Consider these sentences:

> Are you the man **who** wanted to know the time?
> This is the house **that** Jack built.
> I lost the umbrella **which** I had just bought.
> I showed them the book, but they could not tell me
> **whose** it was.
> This is the man **whom** I told you about (about whom
> I told you).

'Who', 'whom', 'whose', 'which', and 'that' are the relative pronouns in these sentences. The table is as follows:

	Persons	Things
Nominative	who	which, that
Accusative	whom	which, that
Genitive	whose	—　　—

The antecedent
The word which the relative pronoun refers back to is known as the **antecedent**.

In the first sentence, 'who' refers to 'man' . . . 'man' is the antecedent.

In the next, 'that' refers to 'house' . . . 'house' is the antecedent.

Next, 'which' refers to 'umbrella' . . . 'umbrella' is the antecedent.

Next, 'whose' refers back to 'book' . . . 'book' is the antecedent.

And, 'whom' refers to 'man' . . . 'man' is the antecedent.

The antecedent may be a whole phrase or sentence. Consider these:

Tom Spencer has made his first million, which shows what you can do when you try. ('Which' refers back to the phrase in bold type.)

He has achieved what he set out to do, which might surprise you. (Here again the antecedent is a whole phrase.)

Two uses of 'which' and 'who' and 'that': defining and non-defining

A rule that can generally be relied upon is to use 'that', without commas, for non-defining clauses and 'which', with two commas, for defining clauses.

'Who', referring to persons, is used in both types of clause.

Consider these two sets of sentences:

1. The lady **who** wore a green dress went shopping.
   The man **who** came to tea left a note.
   The book **that** I bought was damaged.
   The bull **which** was shot yesterday had escaped.
   Any girl **who** carries a torch is safe in the dark.

2. My long-lost brother, **who** arrived home last night, had grown a beard.

My father, **who** works in Scotland, telephoned yesterday.

During the first match of the season, **which** took place yesterday, Danny scored two goals.

The Queen, **who** opened Parliament on Monday, wore the Imperial Crown.

'David Copperfield', **which** was written by Charles Dickens, was made into a film.

In examples (1), the **defining** relative pronoun (in bold) introduces a clause that describes its antecedent as an adjective would:

. . . the green-dress-wearing lady . . .

. . . the came-to-tea man . . .

. . . the bought-by-me book . . .

. . . the shot-yesterday bull . . .

. . . the torch-carrying girl . . .

No commas are necessary in these sentences.

In examples (2), there is no description of the antecedent; it is already defined, precise and identifiable in its own right. What we have is just added information.

. . . 'My brother' is defined as 'long lost'. I am just told incidentally that he 'arrived last night'. Those words do not describe my brother.

. . . 'My father' is an identifiable person. We are just informed that he happens to work in Scotland. Those words do not define my father.

. . . I know that the 'match' was the 'first' one, presumably of the season. That it 'took place yesterday' is information just added.

. . . 'The Queen' needs no description. The fact that she 'opened Parliament' is just another piece of information.

. . . similarly, 'which was written by Charles Dickens' does not describe 'David Copperfield'. It merely adds to the information we have.

In these sentences, where the relative pronoun is used in a **non-defining** way, commas must be used (two).

INTERROGATIVE PRONOUNS ask questions. Their antecedents are *understood*, not stated, e.g.

Who called last night? (Nominative case, subject of 'called')
To **whom** did you give that money? (Accusative case, object of 'to')
What did they do? (Accusative case after 'did do')
Whose is this? (Genitive case)

Note: If, instead of the last sentence, we had written 'Whose book is this?' 'whose' is an **adjective**, which qualifies 'book'. In the sentence 'Whose is this?' it is a **pronoun**, standing for some noun.

The cases of interrogative pronouns are:

Nom:	Who?	What?
Acc:	Whom?	What?
Gen:	Whose?	

Important

Certain usages, which are not strictly grammatically correct, are accepted. E.g.

It's **me**, Dad!
Who should I give it to?
That's **him** over there.

These are permissible colloquialisms.

Summary of the pronoun so far

1. What kind is it?   personal
                      demonstrative
                      relative
                      interrogative

2. What person is it? 1st
                      2nd
                      3rd

3. What gender is it? masculine
                      feminine
                      common
                      neuter

4. What number?   singular
                      plural

5. What case is it?   nominative
                      accusative
                      genitive

6. In the case of relative pronouns, reference should be made to the antecedent.

Exercises

Identify the **pronouns** in these sentences, and say what kind they are. Note that some sentences contain more than one pronoun.

1. What is that you are hiding?
2. I told him that the book was too difficult and he should not try to read it.
3. Look at her! She walks as though she had found a £5 note and then lost it again!
4. Who gave you that money? Why did he do that?
5. The house which we bought was too expensive.
6. I know where he keeps his keys, which he is always mislaying.

7. They said the boy who stole the purse gave it back.
8. Whose is that satchel? You had better give it back to him.
9. Is that chocolate yours? Give me some, please!
10. We saw the pencils and took one. It won't be missed; they have plenty more.

In the following sentences, the **relative pronouns** are set in italics. Say which word, or words, form the antecedent.

1. John, *who* is taller than I am, reached up for me.
2. I gave him the pound *that* I owed him.
3. My football, with the black spot, *which* I lost last week, was found again.
4. It was giving him a black eye *that* made him stop bullying.
5. Be careful, or you'll catch the cold *that* put me to bed last week.
6. I told Sally, *who* was running round the room, to keep still.
7. Our kitten, with its little bell, *that* Dad gave us for a present, ran out into the road.
8. He scored three goals in the match, *which* might astonish all of you.

THE SECOND STEPPING-STONE: NOUNS, PRONOUNS AND ADJECTIVES

Nouns and pronouns identify people, things, places, ideas and groups, but they do not give any descriptive ideas about them.

Queen Elizabeth, goalie, dog, railway-station, beauty, crowd are all nouns, and he, you, it, that are all pronouns, but they don't take us very far.

We often need a more detailed description of these words, and the part of speech used to provide this description is called an **adjective**.

Thus we could say

Our gracious Queen Elizabeth, **the brave** goalie, **my faithful** dog, **the dirty, run-down** railway station, **a strange** beauty, **the noisy** crowd

and

he is **strong** and **brave**, you are **kind** and **thoughtful**, it is **heavy** and **awkward**, that was **nice** and **tasty**

The words in bold are descriptive of the nouns and pronouns to which they refer. They describe them in some detail and make them more meaningful. They are **adjectives**.

Adjectives

Adjective is the name given to words which are used to describe nouns (and, as we shall see later, pronouns). Adjectives enlarge the meaning of nouns, and we say they 'qualify' or 'limit' them. In this book, we shall use the word 'qualify' to describe their function.

For example, 'house' is a noun. An adjective in front of it can tell us more about the house: **large** house, **expensive** house, **dirty** house, **newly-painted** house, **slum-like** house.

The words in bold tell us something more about the word 'house': they qualify it, and describe it in more detail. They are **adjectives.**

What we need to know about **adjectives**

1. What **kind** of adjective is it?

2. What **degree** of comparison does it have?

3. How is it being used (**attributively** or **predicatively**)?

4. What noun does it **qualify**?

KINDS OF ADJECTIVES

1. Descriptive — adjectives showing what qualities a noun has (by far the largest group).

2. Possessive — referring to an individual person, a small, easily identifiable number.

3. Proper   – adjectives derived from proper nouns.

4. Quantitative   – showing quantity: how much, how many.

5. Numeral   – really part of the previous group, but separated because these adjectives derive directly from numbers.

6. Demonstrative – a small group used to point out which particular nouns are being described.

7. Interrogative – adjectives asking which nouns are being referred to.

8. Distributive   – used to separate individual, particular, nouns from a group (a small number, in this section).

Examples of the different **kinds** of adjectives:

Descriptive: a *brave* man, a *comfortable* bed, *fast* cars, a *sweet* face, a *quiet* moment, *happy* children.

Possessive: *my* mother, *their* dog, *our* holiday, *his* pocket-money, *your* uncle, *her* hat, *its* fragrance. ('Its' is a possessive adjective showing that the 'fragrance' belongs to the flower or breeze; a thing, as opposed to the other possessive adjectives, which refer back to people.)

Proper: the *French* language, the *British* empire, *London* town, an *Italian* soldier, a *Gladstone* bag, a *Victorian* coach.

Quantitative: not *much* bread left, *all* the school, *some* buses, *half* the apple, *any* player, not *enough* cakes, *many* men, *several* supporters, a *few*

	people. (These adjectives usually tell us 'how many' or 'how much'.)
Numeral:	*six* apples, *twenty* runs, *eight* pounds, *one* goal, the *third* boy, the *seventh* house, the *first* girl. (Here the reference is to the actual number.)
Demonstrative:	*this* man, *these* women, *that* boy, *those* girls, *such* troubles, *certain* stories, the *same* food, the *other* day. (Demonstrative adjectives 'point out' their nouns.)
Interrogative:	*which* book? *what* car? *whose* money?
Distributive:	*each* day, *every* person, *either* team, *neither* team. ('Each' separate day out of a number of days; 'every' person of those there; 'either' or 'neither' team out of the two.)

ARTICLES

The three words 'a', 'an' and 'the' are special kinds of adjectives.

'A' and 'an' are the **indefinite articles.**
'The' is the **definite article.**

They are always known by these terms, but it is good to remember that they are adjectives because of their function.

Examples of nouns and adjectives used together
(As a help, all **nouns** have been printed in bold type.)

The green **book** belongs to that German **boy** who is studying **science** in the sixth **form.**

My second **son, John,** told his English **teacher** that seven **pages** of poetry **homework** was too much **writing** in one **evening.**

This squirrel-faced **kid** keeps pinching my **sister's** cheese-and-pickle **sandwiches** every **day** and before long I am going to give him some **reward** for his **trouble** that will make him ask, 'What **day** is it?'

To parse these nouns and adjectives, the first thing is to pick out the nouns – which has been done for you. In the first sentence we have '**book**' '**boy**' '**science**' and '**form**'.

Now we ask – what kind of **book**? The answer is 'The green' one. Those two words, 'the' and 'green', describe the book. They are **adjectives.** What kind of **boy**? 'That German' boy is the answer; they, too, are **adjectives.** What kind of **science**? No word here describes 'science'; it has no adjective qualifying it. What kind of **form**? 'The sixth' form is the answer, two more **adjectives.**

To parse these words, **nouns** and **adjectives,** we have to say all we know about them, in the following way:

First sentence

book	common **noun**, neuter, singular
The	**definite article**
green	descriptive **adjective**, qualifying noun 'book'
boy	common **noun**, masculine, singular
that	demonstrative **adjective** qualifying 'boy'
German	proper **adjective**, qualifying 'boy'
science	abstract **noun**, neuter, singular
*form	common **noun** neuter, singular
the	**definite article**
sixth	numeral **adjective**, qualifying 'form'.

*'form' could also be regarded as a **collective noun.**

Second sentence

son	common **noun**, masculine, singular
my	possessive **adjective**, qualifying 'son'
second	numeral **adjective**, qualifying 'son'
John	proper **noun**, masculine, singular
teacher	common **noun**, common gender, singular
his	possessive **adjective**, qualifying 'teacher'
English	proper **adjective**, qualifying 'teacher'
pages	common **noun**, neuter, plural
seven	numeral **adjective**, qualifying 'pages'
homework	common **noun**, neuter, singular
*poetry	descriptive **adjective**, qualifying 'home-work'
writing	common **noun**, neuter, singular
much	quantitative **adjective**, qualifying 'writing'
evening	common **noun**, neuter, singular
one	numeral **adjective**, qualifying 'evening'.

*'poetry' here is an **adjective** because it is *used* as an *adjective*. It qualifies 'homework'. What kind of 'homework'? *Poetry* homework.

On many occasions it is a **noun**: A piece of *poetry*; I am studying *poetry*.

Third sentence

kid	common **noun**, masculine (in this case), singular
this	demonstrative **adjective**, qualifying 'kid'
squirrel-faced	descriptive **adjective**, qualifying 'kid'
sister's	common **noun**, feminine, singular
my	possessive **adjective**, qualifying 'sister's'

sandwiches	common **noun**, neuter, plural
cheese-and-pickle	descriptive **adjective**, qualifying 'sandwiches' (Note: these three words are *one* part of speech)
day	common **noun**, neuter, singular
every	distributive **adjective**, qualifying 'day'
reward	common **noun** (it has some abstract overtones, but the kind of reward the speaker has in mind is probably concrete), neuter, singular
some	quantitative **adjective**, qualifying 'reward'
trouble	abstract **noun** (a less concrete idea than 'reward'), neuter, singular
his	possessive **adjective**, qualifying 'trouble'
day	common **adjective**, neuter, singular
what	interrogative **adjective**, qualifying 'day'.

ATTRIBUTIVE AND PREDICATIVE USES OF ADJECTIVES

Attributive use

Here are some examples:

the **grey** horse	an **expert** sailor
the **out-of-date** diary	a **green** bean
the **clean** plate	the **day-dreaming** student

Note: In the **attributive** use, the adjective comes *in front of* the noun.

Predicative use

Here are some examples:

the horse is **grey**   the sailor is **expert**
the diary is **out of date**   the bean is **green**
the plate is **clean**   the student is **day-dreaming**

Note: In the **predicative** use of the adjective, it is *separated from* its noun by a word like 'is'.

These uses of the adjective can be combined to make sentences more varied:

The old horse is **grey**.
The expert sailor is **tanned**.
The blue diary is **out of date**.
That magic green bean is **mysterious**.
This cracked plate is **clean**.
The young, handsome-looking student is **day-dreaming**.

The words in bold type are **adjectives** or **articles** qualifying the nouns. Those coming before the nouns are said to be used **attributively**; those coming after the nouns, separated by 'is', are used **predicatively**.

Note that some adjectives consist of more than one word, joined by a hyphen: 'day-dreaming', 'handsome-looking'.

Summary of the adjective so far

1. There are eight kinds of adjective:

   descriptive
   possessive
   proper
   quantitative
   numeral
   demonstrative
   interrogative
   distributive.

2. Adjectives qualify nouns (or pronouns).

3. Adjectives can be used attributively
   or predicatively.

Exercises

What kinds of **adjectives** occur in these sentences, and
which **nouns** do they qualify?

We had *a Spanish* omelette for tea.
His jersey was a vivid *red*.
There were *five yellow* dresses in the *front* window.
She gave me too *much* ice-cream for tea.
What a wide-brimmed hat you are wearing!
Each boy has a *small* packet of *bacon-flavoured*
   crisps.
Silly boy, he doesn't know *which* chocolate to take!
This pencil is *black*, but I wanted *a blue* one.
Is this *your* coat?
We'd like *some* soup, please; *two hot* bowlfuls of
   tomato!

Provide a suitable **adjective**, of a kind indicated in the
bracket, in each of these examples:

The (**descriptive**) monster was asleep.

(**demonstrative**) packet of sweets is stale.
(**interrogative**) coat shall I wear today?
The (**proper**) language is not difficult to learn.
I killed (**numeral**) soldiers in the fierce battle.
(**distributive**) man wanted to go swimming.
Tom gave (**possessive**) chocolates to greedy Jane.
Will you have (**quantitative**) money to go shopping?
I don't like (**possessive**) lunch very much.
Ann, put (**demonstrative**) plates on the kitchen
  table, please.

There are six other **adjectives** in the above sentences.
Can you identify them, say what kind they are, and
which nouns they qualify?
  Say which kinds of **adjectives** the words in italics
are, which **nouns** they qualify and whether they are
used **attributively** or **predicatively**.

The *yellow* balls are all *soft*.
These cars would not be allowed on *English* roads.
Pigeons are not usually *tame*.
That policeman asked the *first* man in the bus
  whether he had seen *any* strangers.
Every time *my* school bell rings it sounds *cracked*.
The *two Italian* spies were *hungry* and *dirty*.
Which cake do you like? *The creamy* one or *the French*
  one?
Several questions were *difficult* to answer.
He eats *more* bread than you.

THE THIRD STEPPING-STONE: NOUNS, PRONOUNS AND VERBS

Thus far we have identified people and things (nouns), invented substitute words for them when needed (pronouns), and used other words to describe them and tell us more about them (adjectives).

Nothing much has *happened* yet. Things happen when there is some *action*, when someone *does* something.

We can talk about

My faithful dog   or   the brave goalie

but those two images are static, inactive; they do not operate in any way. They need to be linked with *action words* of some kind. The action words are called **verbs**. This very important part of speech can take many forms, as we shall see. On its own, the verb does not tell us very much:

kicks, told, swam, pokes

These are all verbs, but to fill out their meaning they need nouns or pronouns, together with descriptive adjectives, to convey a complete idea to the reader or listener.

The brave goalie **kicks** the ball out
My faithful dog **swam** across the river

Here the verbs, virtually meaningless by themselves, complete the picture that has been begun by the nouns and adjectives. They tell us what the noun *is doing*, *has done* or *will do*.

Verbs: I

Verbs are words denoting 'action' – 'doing' words – and this is not a bad description, although it is not complete.

'*To swim*' is a **verb**. When you 'swim', you *do* something, an *action* takes place. Used like this, 'swim' is a **verb**.

Nouns and **verbs** need each other. 'Swim', on its own, a **verb**, means very little. 'The boy', on its own, a **noun**, also means very little. But 'The boy swims' makes sense and has meaning. It is a complete sentence.

As a general rule, every sentence in English needs a **noun** (or a **pronoun**, as we shall see) and a **finite verb** to give it meaning.

What we need to know about **verbs**

1. Is it **finite** or **non-finite**?

2. What **kind** of verb is it?

3. What **tense** is it?

4. What **person** is it?

For further aspects of the **verb** (voices, conjugations, moods, etc.) see pp. 67ff.

FINITE OR NON-FINITE

The word '**finite**' means limited, defined in some way.

A *finite* object has borders, it can be measured and related to other objects in certain definite ways. In geometry, a rectangle is a finite figure, it has dimensions which 'fix' it – length and breadth. These are its dimensions.

Non-finite has the opposite meaning. Anything which is *non-finite* has no limits, it can go on for ever. It has no dimensions, it is not fixed or related to other objects. Space is non-finite, it does not begin or end and has no fixed position.

Finite verbs are limited by time and person

In grammar, the limits, or dimensions, are those of time and person (or thing). Just as you need length and breadth to fix a rectangle, so you need the idea of 'time' and a 'person' (or 'thing') to fix a finite verb. Here are some examples:

'I swim'

 The verb is '*swim*' (the *action*)
 The *time* limit is the *Present* (that is *when* I do it)
 The *person* limit is '*I*' ('I' am the *person* who swims)

'John swam'

 The verb is '*swam*' (the *action*)
 The *time* limit is the *Past* (that was *when* I swam – yesterday)
 The *person* limit is '*John*' (*he* did the swimming)

'The car braked'

 The verb is '*braked*' (the *action*)
 The *time* limit is the *Past* (*when* the braking took place)
 The *thing* limit is '*car*' (*it* did the braking)

'The sun will shine' The verb is *'will shine'* (the *action*)

The *time* limit is the *Future* (*when* it will happen)

The *thing* limit is the *'sun'* (*it* will do the shining).

Here are some more examples of **finite verbs:**

'The boy **broke** his toy'

('broke', the verb, is limited by 'boy', the *person*, and the *past time*, when it happened)

'Peter **plays** golf'

('plays', the verb, is limited by 'Peter', the *person*, and the *present time*, when it happens)

'Television **bores** me stiff'

('bores', the verb, is limited by 'television', the *thing* that does the action, and the *present time*, when it takes place)

'Christmas **will come**'

('will come', the verb, is limited by 'Christmas', the *thing or event*, and the *future time*, when it will happen).

We can say, therefore, that **finite verbs** are limited by the two dimensions of *Person* (or *thing*) and *Time* (past, present or future).

Non-finite verbs are not limited by time or person (thing)

If I write 'Swimming is a good exercise', the word 'swimming' gives some idea of action, but it is not a finite verb.

| It is not limited by **time:** | It is not taking place at any particular time. It can be done in the past, the present or the future. There is nothing in this sentence to tell us *when*. |
| It is not limited by **person:** | No particular person is doing it in this sentence. It can apply to anyone. |

In this sentence 'swimming' is **non-finite**, not limited by time or person. In fact, in this sentence, 'swimming' has become a **noun**. It is now the *name* of the action.

The infinitive (and see pp. 76–81 later)

The **infinitive** is a special form of the **non-finite** verb. It is the 'to' form, and verbs are known by this form. It is a kind of label that identifies the verb. 'To swim', 'to learn', 'to dance', 'to shout', 'to write' – all these are **infinitives**; they identify the verb-action. Infinitives can also be used without 'to' in front, as we shall see later.

KINDS OF VERBS

   1. Transitive
   2. Intransitive
   3. Auxiliary

For the time being, we shall look at **transitive** and **intransitive** verbs.

   One pattern for a simple sentence can be this:

| *The doer* | *The action* | *The receiver of the action* |
| (Noun) | (Verb) | (Another noun) |

Examples:

The old man	closed	the door.
My father	punished	my sister.
The stranger	asked	a question.
The bus	hit	the kerb.
The birds	ate	the seeds.

In each of these sentences the 'doer' 'acts' on the 'receiver'. We can prove this by asking a question based on the sentence:

What did the old man close?	the door.
Whom did the father punish?	my sister.
What did the stranger ask?	a question.
What did the bus hit?	the kerb.
What did the birds eat?	the seeds.

The action of the verb is said to be passed from the 'doer' to the 'receiver', and the verbs are described as **transitive**.

Now look at these sentences (the verbs are the same):

The shop	closed	at six o'clock.
The teacher	punished	without mercy.
The stranger	asked	in French.
The angry boy	hit	out wildly.
The young birds	ate	greedily.

Ask the questions again:

What did the shop close?
Whom did the teacher punish?
What did the stranger ask?
What (or whom) did the boy hit?
What did the birds eat?

This time there are no sensible answers, the action does not pass from the 'doer' to the 'receiver'; there simply is no 'receiver'. This is because the verb is used in an **intransitive** way.

Note: It is the way the verb is *used* that matters. The same verb can be **transitive** or **intransitive**, depending on the way it is used in the sentence. For example:

I **stamped** the envelope (transitive)
I **stamped** into the room (intransitive)

Transitive means that the action is passed on to some person or thing that receives it.
Intransitive means that the action is not passed to anyone or any thing.

Note: Two verbs in particular illustrate the importance of the transitive/intransitive uses of the verb: **to lay** and **to lie**.

To lay (to put something somewhere) is *always* transitive.
To lie (to be at rest) is *always* intransitive.

To lay gives us *laid* in the past tense and *laid* in the past participle.
To lie gives us *lay* in the past tense and *lain* in the past participle.

Hence:

Lay: Today I lay the table
Yesterday I laid the table
or I have laid the table

Lie: Today I lie down
        Yesterday I lay down
        or I have lain down

TENSES

Finite verbs always convey a sense of 'time'. Action
can take place:

In the past	*In the present*	*In the future*
(yesterday)	(now)	(tomorrow)

We can say

I swam	I swim	I shall swim
I walked	I walk	I shall walk
I grew	I grow	I shall grow
I met	I meet	I shall meet

Put into a sentence, the **tense** of a verb brings out extra
meaning:

Last week, John Fish **swam** the
    Channel.   (**past** tense)
Tomorrow, I **shall speak** to
    Charlie.   (**future** tense)
Now I **understand** how to parse a
    verb.   (**present** tense)

Note: Verbs can consist of more than one word.

PERSON

In grammar, the word '**person**' is a technical term.
There are three '**persons**': 1st, 2nd and 3rd.

The **1st person** is the one speaking or doing the action.

'I told him off' ('I', the speaker)
'We won the pools' ('We', the people doing the action of 'winning')
'I asked the question' (again, 'I', the speaker)

Because in these sentences it is 'I' or 'we' who do the speaking or take the action, the verbs – 'told', 'won', 'asked' – are also said to be 'in the **1st person**'.

The **2nd person** is the person spoken to, or to whom the action is done.

'You came in late' ('You', the person I am speaking to)
'You hit my brother' (again, the person spoken to)

In a similar way, because 'you' (the person spoken to) is doing the action, the verbs – 'came', 'hit' – are said to be 'in the **2nd person**'.

The **3rd person** is the person or thing spoken about.

'He (that person over there) is very naughty.'
'It (that pane of glass over there) is broken.'
'They (the persons over there) all laughed at me.'
'She (the lady over there) is wearing a nice dress.'

As in the other examples, the verbs here are said to be 'in the **3rd person**': 'is', 'is broken', 'laughed', 'is wearing'.

The small words (**pronouns**) give us the clue to **person**:

I, we: are always **1st person**, and *verbs* used with them will be 'in the **1st person**'.

You (thou): is always **2nd person**, as are the *verbs* used with it.

He, she, it, they and all nouns used with *verbs* are **3rd person**, and the *verbs* used with them are also 'in the **3rd person**'.

Summary of the verb so far

1. Verbs are classified as finite or non-finite.

2. The infinitive is a special form of non-finite verb.

3. A verb can be transitive or intransitive.

4. There are three simple tenses: past, present and future.

5. There are three 'persons': 1st, 2nd and 3rd.

Exercises

Say whether the verbs in italics are **finite** or **non-finite**:

The grey duck *swam* across the river.
Smoking is bad for your health.
The three men *think* they *are* very clever.
I *asked* my mother *to cook* me a kipper.
Walking is *supposed to make* you healthy.
When *going* home, *take* the quickest route.
They *said* they *would go flying* on Tuesday.

Which of the following verbs are **transitive** and which **intransitive**?

Matthew *drew* a picture in his book.
The man in the blue jacket *ran away*.
I *shall knock* your head off!

My favourite subject *is* history.
He *soaked* his shirt in soapy water.
You *are* a coward, I *am* not.
The master *trusted* him to tell the truth.
The doctor *agreed* with his patient about his health.

Say which **tense** the following verbs are in:

I *came* home early yesterday.
The woman *looks* ill.
Children *like* popular music.
During the revolution, the criminal *escaped*.
The Queen *lives* at Buckingham Palace.
I *shall go* to Manchester on Tuesday.
He *went* to Newcastle on Tuesday.
The green jerseys *fitted* the players perfectly.
The silver car *glides* over the road easily.

Which of these verbs are 1st, which 2nd, and which 3rd person?

I *sing* for my supper every night.
He *thinks* he *is* a great cricketer.
He *will be* home at nine o'clock.
We *believe* all pop musicians *are* mad.
They *spoke* quietly because she *was* ill.
You *say* that he *can swim* but I *believe* you *are lying*.

Examine each of the verbs in italics in these sentences and say whether each is **finite** or **non-finite, transitive** or **intransitive**. In addition, give the **tense** and **person** of each verb.

To dance all night *is tiring* for the feet.
The author *tore up* his book because he *thought* *writing was* too difficult for him.
I *shall go* to the concert because I *love to hear* Gazumpski *play* Beethoven.

When Joseph *comes in*, he *shall wash up* all the dishes.

I *don't know* how you *keep* a straight face when Roger *starts to tell* jokes.

Case

The **case** of a noun or pronoun in English grammar is
a definition of its relationship with another word in a
sentence. Normally, the relationship is with a verb or
a preposition.

We shall meet the preposition later p. 58. For the
moment, in dealing with **case**, all we need to know is
that:

Prepositions *govern* nouns and pronouns
They introduce *prepositional phrases*.
Consider these sentences:

1. The boy **sent** a letter to his uncle.
2. After Wednesday you **will have to go** to London.
3. The girls' coats **were** all wet from the rain.
4. John, Mary, Sam and Betty **had spent** their
   money on sweets.
5. I **shall be** captain of the school when you **leave**.

(In each of these sentences the **verbs** are in bold.)

In (1) there are three nouns: 'boy', 'letter', 'uncle'.

'Boy' relates to 'sent'. The boy did the sending. 'Boy'
therefore is the **subject** of 'sent'.
'Letter' also relates to 'sent'. It is the object that was
sent by the boy. It is the **object** of 'sent'.
The third noun, 'uncle', relates to the word 'to'. 'To
his uncle' is a prepositional phrase. 'Uncle'
therefore is **governed by** the preposition 'to'.

In (2) there are two nouns, 'Wednesday' and 'London',
and one pronoun, 'you'.

'Wednesday' is part of the prepositional phrase 'After Wednesday', and it is **governed by** 'after'.

'London' similarly is part of 'to London'. It is **governed by** 'to'.

'You' relates to 'will have to go'. 'You' are the person who will have to do the going, 'you' is the **subject** of 'will have to go'.

In (3) there are three nouns: 'girls'', 'coats', and 'rain'.

'Coats' relates to 'were'. It is the **subject** of 'were'.

'Rain' is part of the phrase 'from the rain'. It is **governed by** 'from'.

'Girls'' shows **possession**. We understand that the coats belong to the girls.

In (4) there arc six nouns: 'John', 'Mary', 'Sam', 'Betty', 'money' and 'sweets'.

The four people did the spending, so each one is a **subject** of the verb 'had spent'.

'Money' also relates to 'had spent', it tells us what had been spent, it is the **object** of the spending.

'Sweets' is part of the short phrase 'on sweets'. It is **governed by** the preposition 'on'.

In (5) there is one noun, 'captain', and two pronouns: 'I' and 'you'.

'I' is the one who shall be, the **subject**.

'You' is the **subject** of the verb 'leave'; 'you' will be the one leaving.

'Captain' relates to 'I'; they are the same person. 'Captain' is a complement to 'I', and so it shares its **subject** status.

'School' is part of the phrase 'of the school'; it is the **object** of the preposition 'of'.

It will be seen that three relationships have emerged: **subject, object** and **possession**. These correspond to the three cases in grammar.

Subject words are said to be in the **nominative case**. **Object** words are said to be in the **accusative case**, and words indicating **possession** are said to be in the **genitive case**. (Other terms used for these cases are Subjective, Objective and Possessive.)

Ghosts of the past are sometimes met in connection with cases. Vocative and Dative may still haunt the jargon. Dative still occurs in German and Latin grammars. These terms are not widely used in English grammar today, although some practitioners are loyal to them.

NOMINATIVE CASE

As subject: **Tom Brown** ran away.
                     Six **soldiers** manned the gun.
As complement: You are the **man** to go.
                     He was an **engineer**.
In apposition: The doctor, **Dr Jones**, called to see the invalid.
                     My sister, **Anne Marie**, is a very beautiful girl.

ACCUSATIVE CASE

As object: Mr Thomas teaches **French**.
                     I made an **apple pie**.
After a preposition: He called me *into* the **house**.
                     Before the **party**, I went home to change *into* **evening dress**.

Adverbial accusatives

Consider these sentences:

> I spent eight **nights** in Spain   (time)
> She ran twenty **miles** in the marathon (place)
> The book cost five **pounds**   (how much).

The words, 'nights', 'miles', 'pounds', could be described as **adverbial accusatives** because of the time and place associations they evoke. The sentences can also be expanded as follows:

> I spent (a period of) eight nights in Spain . . .
> She ran (a distance of) twenty miles . . .
> The book cost (the sum of) five pounds.

Many of the sentences we use are condensed in this way, but by expanding their meaning fully, we now see that 'nights', 'miles' and 'pounds' are nouns in the accusative case because they are **governed by** the preposition 'of'.

Retained accusative

In the passive voice we may meet sentences like these:

> The girls were taught elocution.
> The women were brought some coffee and tea.

In the passive, the action of the verb is directed to the **subject**; there cannot be an 'object' of a passive verb in the normal sense. It will be seen that, in sentences like these, 'elocution' is a kind of object of 'taught', and 'coffee and tea' an object of 'were brought'. These words are known as 'retained objects' and are in the **accusative case** for that reason.

Indirect object (i.e. the dative case)

Consider these sentences:

> The master teaches his pupils **maths**.
> I gave my son **sixpence**.

It can be seen that 'maths' and 'sixpence' are nouns in the accusative case, objects of the verbs 'teaches' and 'gave'.

When we come to look at 'pupils' and 'my son', we can rewrite the sentences like this:

> The master teaches maths **to his pupils**.
> I gave sixpence **to my son**.

'Pupils' and 'son' are in the accusative case here governed by the word 'to'. In the original sentences, we can regard them as 'indirect objects' of the verbs.

GENITIVE CASE

The **genitive case**, which shows possession, is one of the very few instances in modern English of words retaining inflexions as a result of usage. The rule is simple:

> Where a noun needs to indicate possession, 's (apostrophe s) is added to the word in the singular and s' (s apostrophe) in the plural.

Thus: John's book (the book belonging to John).
       Mr Harris's car.
       The church's spire.
       The country's flag.
       The boy's commonsense.

And in the plural: The girls' coats.
                    The horses' tails.
                    The saucepans' lids.
                    The schoolmistresses' handbags.

Note: Where plural words end in a letter other than 's', only 's will be added: The men's shorts. The children's shoes.

Its and it's

When the pronoun 'it' is used to show possession, it is written **without** the apostrophe: Its.

e.g. The bottle lost **its** top.
After the gale hit the tree, all **its** leaves blew off.
The train sounded **its** whistle.

It's is an abbreviation of either **it is** or **it has**, and is used only in this way.

e.g. **It's** no use crying. (It is . . .)
Put that down. You don't know where **it's** been. (It has . . .)
Well, **it's** raining again. (It is . . .)

Exercises
Nouns and **pronouns** in the following sentences have been set in italics for you. State which **case** each one is in.

If the word is in the **nominative** case, indicate which **verb** it is the subject of.

If the word is in the **accusative** case, state whether it is the object of a **verb**, and which verb that is, or whether it is **governed** by a preposition, and say which one.

Here are some examples:

John gave the **book** to his **teacher**.
John – nom. case, subject of 'gave'.
book – acc. case, object of 'gave'.
teacher – acc. case, governed by prep. 'to'.

I told my **mother** that **Bill** would not be home until **Uncle Jim** brought **him** in his **car**.

I (pron.) – nom. case, subject of 'told'.

mother (noun) – acc. case, object of 'told'.

Bill (noun) – nom. case, subject of 'would . . . be home'.

Uncle Jim (noun) – nom. case, subject of 'brought'.

him (pron.) – acc. case, object of 'brought'.

car (noun) – acc. case, governed by prep. 'in'.

1. The *sun* shone over the *country* for six *hours* yesterday.
2. If *George* comes home early, *you* tell *him* *he* should take his *tea* *himself*.
3. *Sally's* *aunt* has a *hair-style* *that* doesn't suit *her*.
4. *England* will not give up her *independence* for *anyone*.
5. If *I* lend *you* a *pound*, when shall *I* see *it* again?
6. *They* took some *sweets*, but there is still *one* left for *you*.
7. *Scotland's* *fishing-fleets* catch *tons* of *mackerel* in the *North Sea*.
8. *Mr Choppem*, the *butcher*, gave *Mother* a *piece* of *beef* for *dinner*.
9. *I* was given a *cup* of hot *chocolate* by *nurse* after the *operation*.
10. Tell *me*, where has the *dog* hidden his *bone*?

THE FOURTH STEPPING-STONE: VERBS AND ADVERBS

One of the joys of grammar is the building-block syndrome, the different parts of speech fitting together with pattern and purpose to convey precise or picturesque meaning.

As might be expected from the terms themselves, **verb** and **adverb** are closely related. An **adverb** extends the meaning of a **verb** in much the same way as an **adjective** helps to enlarge the meaning of a **noun**. If we begin with a statement such as 'sailor left', we have the barest outline of an idea.

If we add an adjective to the noun **sailor**, we might get 'The newly-married sailor left.'

We begin to see a clearer picture. If we now enlarge the verb *left* (that is what he *did*), 'yesterday the newly-married sailor left reluctantly', we know now **when** he left (yesterday) and **how** he left (reluctantly), and these **adverbs** help us to understand the verb idea (*left*) with much more insight.

In this way, the meaning of the **verb** is extended, or modified, by the **adverbs** associated with it.

Adverbs

Adverbs, as their name shows, add something to the meaning of a **verb**. We can write: 'The train arrived', a sentence where 'arrived' is the verb. We can also write: 'The train arrived **early**', or 'The train arrived **late**'. 'Early' and 'late' add to the meaning of the verb 'arrived'. They are **adverbs**.

We say adverbs **modify** verbs (also, as we shall see, they modify adjectives and other adverbs). Thus, in the sentence: 'The train arrived *early*', 'early' is an adverb **modifying** the verb 'arrived'.

> What we need to know about **adverbs**
>
> 1. Kinds of adverbs.
>
> 2. What other word, or words, in the sentence the adverb relates to, or modifies.
>
> 3. Degree of comparison.

KINDS OF ADVERBS

1. Of **time** (answering the question 'When?')
2. Of **place** (answering the question 'Where?')
3. Of **manner** (answering the question 'How?' 'In what way?')
4. Of **number** (answering the question 'How many times?')
5. Of **degree** (answering the question 'To what extent?')
6. Of **reason** (answering the question 'Why?' or 'For what reason?')

7. Of **condition** (Introduced usually by 'If' or 'Whether')
8. Of **concession** (Introduced usually by 'though' or 'although')
9. **Affirmation** or **negation** ('yes' and 'no', 'not')

Note: Many adverbs can also be used **interrogatively**, to ask questions.

Examples of adverbs used to **modify** the meaning of verbs:

I shall **soon** be home. The plane has **already** landed. (time)
Here is your supper. It was **nowhere** to be found. (place)
I slept **soundly**. John will **gladly** baby-sit. (manner)
The car skidded **twice**. **Once** I found a Roman coin. (number)
Teacher was **rather** pleased. He **almost** touched the bar. (degree)
Why did he telephone? (reason, but also interrogative)
I shall play football **if** my kit is ready. (condition)
Though he is late, I shall not mind. (concession)
She can **certainly** cook. I did **not** steal it. (affirmation and negation)

Use of adverbs to modify meaning of adjectives

Consider these sentences:

She was **happy**. ('happy' is an adjective, qualifying 'she')
The car was **perfect**. ('perfect' is an adjective, qualifying 'car')
John is a **clever** boy. ('clever' is an adjective, qualifying 'boy')

Each of these adjectives can have an adverb placed before it which modifies its meaning in some way:

She was **blissfully** happy. ('Blissfully' tells us **how** happy she was)

The car was **almost** perfect. ('almost' tells us **to what degree** it was perfect)

John is a **very** clever boy. ('very' tells us **how** clever John was)

These adverbs are said to **modify** the adjectives that follow them.

Use of adverbs to modify the meaning of other adverbs

Consider these sentences:

The train travelled **slowly**. ('slowly' – adverb modifying 'travelled')

Suddenly the dog appeared. ('suddenly' – adverb modifying 'appeared')

He speaks French **well**. ('well' – adverb modifying 'speaks')

Now observe how other adverbs can be used to modify those already in the sentences:

The train travelled **very** slowly. (How slowly? – *very* slowly)

Quite suddenly the dog appeared. (How suddenly? – *quite* suddenly)

He speaks French **particularly** well. (How well? – *particularly* well)

'Yes', 'no' and 'not' are regarded as adverbs.

Yes, I want some more, please. (**affirmation**)

No, he is **not** coming today. (**negation**)

Note: 'Not' comes between parts of compound verbs:

He is walking to London – He is **not** walking to London.
I shall be bringing your lunch – I shall **not** be bringing your lunch.

Summary of the adverb so far

1. What kind is it?
   time
   place
   manner
   number
   degree
   reason
   condition
   concession
   affirmation or negation

2. What other part of speech does it modify?
   verb
   adjective
   other adverb

Exercises
Pick out the **adverbs** in these sentences and say what kinds they are:

1. Cleverly he steered his car through the traffic.
2. Why ask me where the food is kept?
3. I did not know he was Russian.
4. He frequently flies first-class to New York.
5. She played the piece beautifully.
6. Rarely have I seen him so angry.
7. Yes, I think you walked terribly dangerously near the edge of the cliff.

8. Hopefully he will exchange that badly-made machine.
9. Lastly, I want you to make absolutely sure that the children go to bed early and brush their teeth properly.
10. I told him twice and repeated it again, but he did not listen carefully to me.

Put an **adverb** in the blank spaces in these sentences to make sense of what is written.

1. He was . . . late for school.
2. I am . . . sure if I can . . . come to the party.
3. The . . . wounded man died the next day.
4. He tied the parcel . . . and it fell apart in the post.
5. I don't know . . . he went to the U.S.A.
6. John Brown will be . . . missed by his family.
7. Tell me . . . you are going . . .
8. Roger was . . . dirty when he came home.
9. Everyone was . . . relieved to hear of the rescue.
10. The tree trunk was . . . covered over by leaves.

COMPARISON OF ADJECTIVES AND ADVERBS

There are three **degrees of comparison** in English grammar when using adjectives and adverbs:

positive
comparative
superlative

Adjectives

The normal use of an adjective is in the **positive** degree:

The boy is **tall.** The **big** man. We sat at the **long** table.

When we compare **two** things, we need to use the **comparative** degree:

This boy is **tall**, that boy is **taller.**
The **big** man, the **bigger** man.
We sat at the **long** table, we sat at the **longer** table.

If we compare **more than two** things, we need the **superlative** degree:

This boy is **tall,** that boy is **taller**, the other one is **tallest.**
The **big** man, the **bigger** man, the **biggest** man.
We sat at the **long** table, . . . the **longer** table, . . . the **longest** table.

Adjectives of two or more syllables:

Positive	Comparative	Superlative
beautiful	more beautiful	most beautiful
generous	more generous	most generous
ignorant	more ignorant	most ignorant

Some exceptions:

bad, worse, worst	good, better, best
little, less, least	many, more, most
much, more, most	

Adverbs

Adverbs are compared in the same way as adjectives. As most adverbs are more than one syllable, the 'more' and 'most' forms have to be used. For example:

Positive	*Comparative*	*Superlative*
bitterly	more bitterly	most bitterly
clearly	more clearly	most clearly
quickly	more quickly	most quickly

Note:

early, earlier, earliest   fast, faster, fastest
long, longer, longest   soon, sooner, soonest

Some exceptions:

badly, worse, worst   far, farther, farthest
    (or further, furthest)
ill, worse, worst   late, later, latest or last
much, more, most   well, better, best

Consider these sentences:

> Of the three soldiers, John Brown acted **most bravely** in the battle.
> It was the **worst** storm we had ever experienced.
> Of all the children in the class, Betty worked **most willingly**.

Avoid

If there are only two things being compared, the superlative **must not** be used. These sentences are **wrong:**

> Harry was the *tallest* of the two. (**taller**)
> I had the *biggest* of the two ice-creams. (**bigger**)
> Give me the *longest* of those two sticks. (**longer**)

THE FIFTH STEPPING-STONE: NOUNS, PRONOUNS, VERBS AND PREPOSITIONS AND CONJUNCTIONS

The close interdependence of the parts of speech we have considered so far can be further extended by the use of two more, **prepositions** and **conjunctions**. These very common, often quite small, words act as catalysts in sentences.

Consider these basic components of a statement:

Mother put some sugar the bowl placed it the table.

If someone said that, you would probably scratch your head for a moment, but might then understand what was meant. A number of small words had been omitted:

Mother put some sugar **in** the bowl **and** placed it **on** the table.

Here are two more examples:

You go bed go see Mary is asleep her cot.
The bridge the man the army uniform put a bomb the dustbin ran the waiting car.

We obviously need to supply the small words:

Before you go **to** bed, go **in and** see **if** Mary is asleep **in** her cot.
Under the bridge the man **in** the army uniform put a bomb **in** the dustbin **and** ran **to** the waiting car.

Some of these small words are **prepositions** and some are **conjunctions**. They are the last of the building blocks that keep the parsing structure in place.

Prepositions

Prepositions define a relationship between two other parts of speech. It may be between a noun/pronoun and a verb, or two noun/pronoun ideas.

Consider these sentences:

1. The boy kicked the football **into** the goal.
2. The mouse was caught **in** the trap.
3. The prisoner stood **before** the judge.

In (1), 'into' links the two words 'football' and 'goal', two nouns.

In (2), 'in' brings together 'was caught' and 'trap', a verb and a noun.

In (3), 'before' gives the position of the 'prisoner' in relation to the 'judge', again two nouns.

It is worth observing that in each of these sentences the verbal idea also contributes to the relationship between the words:

kicked into . . .
caught in . . .
stood before . . .

What we need to know about **prepositions**

Very little. Prepositions are said to '**govern**' the nouns or pronouns that follow them in the accusative case.

Thus, in the sentences above:

In (1), '**into**' governs 'goal', and 'goal' is in the accusative case.

In (2), '**in**' governs the word 'trap' in the accusative case.

In (3), '**before**' governs the word 'judge' in the accusative case.

Prepositional phrases

A preposition normally introduces a short group of words, two or three, to form a prepositional phrase:

in the garden, **over** the wall, **after** the game, **by** train, **with** me, **without** a smile, **on** a bicycle, **for** example.

COMMON PREPOSITIONS

by, with, on, at, for, to, in, around, under, over, except, from, without, of, upon, across, until, between, during, near.

Prepositions and verbs

Care has to be taken in choosing the correct preposition to follow a verb. Here are some common examples to remember:

to agree **with** (someone)
to agree **to** (something)
to change **for** (something)
to comment **on**
to complain **of**
to be conscious **of**
to despair **of**
to die **for** (someone)

to be indignant **at** (something)
to be indignant **with** (someone)
to be inspired **by**
to interfere **with**
to meddle **with**
to part **from** (somebody)
to part **with** (something)

to die **of** (something)

to differ **from** (an opinion)

to differ **with** (a person)

to disagree **with**

to be disappointed **in** (something)

to be disappointed **with** (someone)

to be disgusted **at** (something)

to be disgusted **with** (someone)

to be equal **to**

to be filled **with**

to protest **against**

to recoil **from**

to rely **on**

to suffer **from**

to tire **of**

to thirst **for** or **after**

to wait **for** (person, thing)

to wait **upon** (someone)

to write **about** (something)

to write **to** (someone)

Other kinds of objects

Prepositions can govern a variety of parts of speech in addition to nouns and pronouns. Here are some examples:

I hope to be home **by** *then* (adverb)

The station is a mile **from** *here* (adverb)

The concert should have finished **before** *now* (adverb)

You can't expect your pen to last **for** *ever* (adverb)

He was **about** *to fly* to America (infinitive)

She did nothing **but** *count* her money (infinitive)

Don't talk to her again **until** *at least a month has passed* (clause)

In sentences like these it is possible to parse 'then', 'here', 'now', 'ever', as nouns, names of times or places in their own right. Even as pronouns. This legitimates the preposition-noun relationship. The infinitives, too, are parts of a verb used as a noun see p. 77.

Note: Prepositions are sometimes omitted, but their presence has to be understood:

Four o'clock = four *of* the clock
Fifty pence a basket = fifty pence *for* a basket
Mother comes to visit us twice a month = . . . twice
in a month.

Summary of the preposition

Prepositions govern other parts of speech, normally nouns and pronouns, in the accusative case.

Prepositions show a relationship between two other words, or phrases, in a sentence.

Conjunctions

As the name suggests, **conjunctions** are joining words. They link single words or longer groups of words, which naturally join together to express a whole idea.

What we need to know about **conjunctions**

1. What **kind** is it?
2. What words, phrases or clauses are **joined**?

KINDS OF CONJUNCTIONS

Co-ordinating: joining words and phrases of **equal** status.

Subordinating: joining principal to **subordinate** clauses.

Co-ordinating conjunctions

Consider these sentences:

1. Joan **and** Tom went cycling.
2. Shall I wear my mac **or** my coat?
3. Mr Jones is very clever **but** he is not conceited.
4. You have not done your homework, **nor** have you eaten your tea.

It will be seen that the words in bold (the conjunctions) join together words (nos 1 and 2) or clauses (nos 3 and 4) that arc equal in function.

in (1) 'Joan' and 'Tom'

in (2) 'mac' or 'coat'

in (3) 'Mr Jones is very clever' and 'he is not conceited'

in (4) The two complete clauses in the sentence.

Subordinating conjunctions

Consider these sentences:

1. John stated very clearly **that** he was not coming back.
2. She will have to leave the school **because** she has behaved so badly.
3. The man looked for a new job **so that** he could earn more money.
4. **If** you are attacked, defend yourself with this revolver.
5. **Although** Tommy was late, the master let him off.
6. I am not as rich **as** you are.
7. Bill is richer **than** either of us is.
8. Mother said she would make tea **after** she had finished her sewing.

First, one can see that the **conjunction** introduces part of a sentence which is subordinate to the other part – it depends on it.

in (1), 'that he was not coming back' simply tells us what he stated very clearly.

in (2), 'because she has behaved so badly' gives us the reason she will have to leave school.

in (3), again, 'so that he can earn more money' tells us why the man looked for a new job.

In the remaining sentences, the main parts of the sentences are 'the master let him off', 'I am not as rich', 'Bill is richer' and 'Mother said she would make tea'. The other parts, introduced by the conjunctions, are subordinate.

Secondly, it will be seen that some of the conjunctions have an adverbial sense in their usage:

(2) '**because** she has behaved so badly' – adverb of **reason**

(4) '**if** you are attacked' – adverb of **condition**

(5) '**although** Tommy was late' – adverb of **concession**

(8) '. . . **after** she finished her sewing' – adverb of **time**.

It will be seen later that part of the function of these conjunctions is to introduce adverbial clauses, hence the association.

Summary of the conjunction

1. Conjunctions are essentially joining words.

2. They co-ordinate one idea with another or subordinate one idea to another.

Exercises on prepositions and conjunctions
Underline all the **prepositional phrases** in these sentences:

1. Without looking, he crossed over to the station.
2. My father, after retiring, used to play golf for two days a week.
3. She saw a lovely dress in the window, and looked in her purse to see if she had enough money.

4. Outside the shop, there was a sign with a large red cross in the middle of a blue square.
5. Give the package with the coloured string to Mrs Jones and the one in the blue bag to Henry.
6. Over the wall I could see two birds in a nest with their chicks under a leafy branch.
7. Mother won't be home until six o'clock. Start tea without her.
8. During the summer we rent a caravan near the sea, just off the coast of North Wales.
9. From where I am standing I can see three ships in the distance, about two miles away.
10. We'll walk across the moors and pick some flowers for Cathy.

Pick out the **conjunctions** used in these sentences, and say whether they are co-ordinating or subordinating conjunctions:

1. My brother and sister are older than I am.
2. I shall go to Scouts after I have finished my tea.
3. Do you want coffee or tea for lunch?
4. If Tommy calls for me, tell him I've gone out.
5. My dog is very small but he can run as fast as yours.
6. Our school is not as big as yours.
7. The train won't leave until all the baggage is aboard.
8. The planes could not take off because the ice was too thick on the runway.
9. John, Bill and George went swimming in the river.
10. The mistress told the girls that they had worked very well.

Interjections

Hardly a part of speech, the **interjection** is simply the recording of a sound, such as:

    Oh!   Ah!   Ha! Ha!   Ouch!   Psst!

and odd sounds of exclamation, such as:

    Bravo!   Cheers!   What-ho!   Hello!

It needs no more than identification as an **interjection**, without any reference to function or relationship in the sentence.

Verbs: II

In previous sections we have discussed the following aspects of the verb:

Finite and non-finite forms of the verb
The infinitive
Past, present and future tenses
1st, 2nd and 3rd person
Transitive and intransitive forms.

There are further aspects of the verb to be studied, including:

Active and passive voices
Conjugations
Further tense formations
Indicative, infinitive, imperative and subjunctive moods
Participles, present, past and perfect
Gerunds (verbal nouns)
Strong and weak verbs

A Table of the Verb, giving an overview of all possible forms the verb idea can assume, is on pp. 72–4.

USEFUL DEFINITIONS USED IN THE STUDY OF VERBS

Active and passive voices

Active: the subject performs the action: The man fed the dog.

Passive: the subject suffers the action: The dog was fed by the man.

Conjugation of verbs
A complete set of verb forms for all persons, singular and plural. To conjugate the verb 'to sing' in the present tense, we write:

1st pers. I sing
2nd pers. You sing (thou singest) Singular
3rd pers. He, she, it sings

1st pers. We sing
2nd pers. You sing Plural
3rd pers. They sing

Participle
Non-finite part of verb, in -ing or -ed, used for constructing tenses, or as an adjective.

Gerund
A form of the verb, ending in -ing, used as a noun, sometimes called a verbal noun.

Infinitive
The 'to . . .' form of the verb. 'To dance', 'To argue' 'To laugh'. Sometimes 'to' is omitted.

Inflexion
A change in the form of a verb for grammatical purposes:

walk, walks, walking, walked.

Mood
Changes in meanings of verb forms. There are four **moods:**

indicative infinitive imperative subjunctive.

The indicative mood is the mood of **statement.**
The imperative mood is the one of **command** or **order.**
The subjunctive mood is the one of **doubt, suspicion** or **fear.**
The infinitive mood is the 'to . . .' form.

Finite verb
Part of the verb limited by time and person.

Person
1st, 2nd and 3rd person, as already defined.

Strong and weak verbs
Strong verbs alter vowels when inflected: I swim, I swam.
Weak verbs do not alter vowels: I play, I played.

ACTIVE AND PASSIVE VOICES

Verbs are put into one of two voices, or categories, according to whether the subject executes the action of the verb or 'suffers' it. (The word 'suffer' is used here as it corresponds to the meaning of the Latin root of 'passive'.)

Here are some examples where the subject executes the action:

The man *struck* a blow.
Tom *filled* the jug.
He *spoke* French.

If we rewrite these sentences so that the subject 'suffers' the action, we shall get:

A blow *was struck* by the man.
The jug *was filled* by Tom.
French *was spoken* by him.

'Struck', 'filled' and 'spoke' are said to be in the **active voice.**
'Was struck', 'was filled' and 'was spoken' are in the **passive voice.**

It will be seen that the passive voice is formed by using tenses of the auxiliary verb 'to be'. A full table of both active and passive voices is given in the synopses on pp. 72–4.

TENSE

The **tense** of a verb gives its position in time.

English grammar is particularly well endowed to provide subtle gradations of time sequences for its verbs, as the following table will show.

Verb: **to tell**

active voice

Tense	Completed time	Continuous time
Past perfect (pluperfect)	I had told	I had been telling
Perfect	I have told	I have been telling
Past (imperfect)	I told	I was telling
Present	I tell	I am telling
Future	I shall tell	I shall be telling
Future perfect	I shall have told	I shall have been telling
Conditional	I should tell	I should be telling
Past conditional	I should have told	I should have been telling

passive voice

Tense	Completed time	Continuous time
Past perfect	I had been told	–
Perfect	I have been told	–
Past	I was told	I was being told
Present	I am told	I am being told
Future	I shall be told	–
Future perfect	I shall have been told	–
Conditional	I should be told	–
Past conditional	I should have been told	–

Note: The **perfect tenses** convey a sense of an action that is completed, finished once and for all.

The **continuous tenses** convey the sense that the action was, is, will be continuing for a period of time, was, is, will be on-going for a time.

Following this, the verb 'to tell' will be conjugated in all its voices in both singular and plural.

Verb: **to tell** (indicative mood, active voice)

	Past perfect	Continuous	Perfect	Continuous
Sing.	1. I had told	I had been telling	I have told	I have been telling
	2. You had told	You had been telling	You have told	You have been telling
	3. He had told	He had been telling	He has told	He has been telling
Pl.	1. We had told	We had been telling	We have told	We have been telling
	2. You had told	You had been telling	You have told	You have been telling
	3. They had told	They had been telling	They have told	They have been telling

	Past	Past continuous	Present	Present continuous
Sing.	1. I told	I was telling	I tell	I am telling
	2. You told	You were telling	You tell	You are telling
	3. He told	He was telling	He tells	He is telling
Pl.	1. We told	We were telling	We tell	We are telling
	2. You told	You were telling	You tell	You are telling
	3. They told	They were telling	They tell	They are telling

	Future	Future continuous	Future perfect	Future perfect cont.
Sing.	1. I shall tell	I shall be telling	I shall have told	I shall have been telling
	2. You will tell	You will be telling	You will have told	You will have been telling
	3. He will tell	He will be telling	He will have told	He will have been telling
Pl.	1. We shall tell	We shall be telling	We shall have told	We shall have been telling
	2. You will tell	You will be telling	You will have told	You will have been telling
	3. They will tell	They will be telling	They will have told	They will have been telling

Verb: **to tell** (indicative mood, passive voice)

	Past perfect	Perfect
Sing.	1. I had been told	I have been told
	2. You had been told	You have been told
	3. He had been told	He has been told
Pl.	1. We had been told	We have been told
	2. You had been told	You have been told
	3. They had been told	They have been told

		Past	Past continuous	Present	Present continuous
Sing.	1.	I was told	I was being told	I am told	I am being told
	2.	You were told	You were being told	You are told	You are being told
	3.	He was told	He was being told	He is told	He is being told
Pl.	1.	We were told	We were being told	We are told	We are being told
	2.	You were told	You were being told	You are told	You are being told
	3.	They were told	They were being told	They are told	They are being told

		Future	Future perfect
Sing.	1.	I shall be told	I shall have been told
	2.	You will be told	You will have been told
	3.	He will be told	He will have been told
Pl.	1.	We shall be told	We shall have been told
	2.	You will be told	You will have been told
	3.	They will be told	They will have been told

Note: There are no continuous tenses in the past perfect, perfect, future or future perfect in the passive voice.

Conditional tenses

Active voice

Future conditional	*Future cond. continuous*
1. I should tell	I should be telling.
2. You would tell	You would be telling.
3. He would tell	He would be telling.
1. We should tell	We should be telling.
2. You would tell	You would be telling.
3. They would tell	They would be telling.

Passive voice

Future conditional

1. I should be told.
2. You would be told.
3. He would be told.

1. We should be told.
2. You would be told.
3. They would be told.

Note: There is no continuous tense of the future conditional in the passive voice.

MOODS

Verbal ideas are expressed in one of four moods:

Indicative, infinitive, imperative, subjunctive

Indicative mood

This is the 'normal' form of the mood, used when the verbal idea is part of a statement being expressed by the writer.

Infinitive mood

This form is not declined; it has no attachment to person or number.

It is often found in the 'to . . .' form, and verbal ideas expressed in this way are always infinitives. E.g.

I intend **to see** that film.
John liked **to listen** to jazz.
To climb Everest is my ambition.

It is also found without the prefix 'to'. E.g.

I saw them **walk** in the road.
The supermarkets make you **buy** their goods.
Did you watch Arsenal **play** Spurs?
They felt the wind **beat** against the door.

<u>What we need to know about the **infinitive**</u>

1. What **kind** is it?
2. What is its **use** in the sentence?

Kinds of infinitives

The infinitive can take any one of the following forms:

	Active	**Passive**
Present	to tell	to be told
Pres. cont.	to be telling	–

Perfect	to have told	to have been told
Perfect cont.	to have been telling	–

Note 1: The **future** can be expressed only by using a phrase such as 'To be about to tell' or 'To be going to tell', but these are **not** future infinitive forms of 'to tell'.

Note 2: After certain verbs – those expressing wish, intention or duty – the perfect form of the infinitive is used to show that the wish or intention was *not* carried out. E.g.

He intended **to have paid** me (but he did not).
He ought **to have listened** to your advice (but he did not).
He wanted **to have stayed** the night (but he did not).

Uses of infinitive mood

The **infinitive** can be used:

1. As a **noun**
   (a) As a **subject** of a verb (in the nominative case):

   To climb Everest is my ambition.
   To gather rosebuds while you may is my advice.
   To drink and drive is a very foolish mistake.

   (b) As the **object** of a preposition (in the accusative case):

   The Prince was **about to launch** the boat.
   He was **about to be attacked** by the mob.
   You were **near to driving** over the cliff.

(c) As a **complement**:

> Talking to him is **to waste** your words.
> John seems **to be** quite intelligent.
> My sister is **to appear** in a ballet.

2. As an **adjective**

> I want a ball **to play** football with.
> He gave me a piece of chocolate **to eat**.
> The meat was **to be cooked** that day.

3. As an **adverb**

> He visited his grandfather **to see** how he was.
> (Why?)
> He shouted **to attract** their attention. (For
> what reason?)
> My father worked **to earn** his living. Why?

The split infinitive

In English usage the infinitive can comprise two, three
or even four words and there are occasions when
infiltrators, usually in the form of adverbs, invade its
structure and 'split' it.
Consider:

> She seemed **to** *rather* **fancy** that blue hat.
> The boy had **to** *finally* **come** home to his family.

The infiltrators, *rather* and *finally*, have split the
infinitives **to fancy** and **to come**. The question is, is
this grammatically permissible? In the case of the
perfect infinitive, examples such as these are not
uncommon:

> He claims **to have** *never previously* **seen** Paris.

The man pretends **to have** *always before* **been regarded** as a loyal worker.

If we accept that infinitives must never be split, the above sentences will have to be rewritten as follows:

She seemed rather **to fancy** that blue hat.
The boy had finally **to come** home to his family.
He claims never **to have seen** Paris previously.
The man pretends always before **to have been regarded** as a loyal worker.

These are stilted and artificial sentences but they are correct. No. 3 is perhaps the most acceptable, but the others have to be described, at best, as literary.

The 'never-split-the-infinitive' position is a clumsy and often a non-idiomatic device to try to preserve what is primarily a laudable object, one which has much logic on its side. It rarely, however, 'sounds' right. To advise students on this matter one might say:

The general rule that infinitives should not be split is sound and must generally be observed.

In colloquial use there are occasions when splitting can be winked at. The first sentence above is a fair example of this.

Where one is in difficulty, the wisest course is to recast the sentence, e.g.

Finally, the boy had **to come** home to his family.
He claims that he had never before been to Paris (infinitive dispensed with).
The man pretends that previously he had always been regarded as a loyal worker (again, infinitive dispensed with).

Note: Although **infinitives** are used as nouns, adjectives or adverbs, they retain some of their verbal powers. They can, for example, have objects of their own:

I wanted **to kick** the ball.
'To kick' is itself a noun-equivalent, object of what
    I wanted. But it also has its own object: 'the ball'.

The teacher tried **to teach** his class how **to cook**
    cabbage.
'To teach' has an object: 'his class'.
'To cook' has an object: 'cabbage'.

Summary of infinitive mood

Kinds of infinitives

> Active: Present and present continuous.
>   Perfect and perfect continuous.
>
> Passive: Present and perfect.

Function

> Used as a **noun** – subject
>   object
>   complement
>   after a preposition.
>
> Used as an **adjective**.
> Used as an **adverb**.

Mention should also be made if the **infinitive**
has any object of its own.

Exercises on the infinitive
State what kinds of **infinitives** the following are:

1. *To be lying* in bed so late is bad.

2. I would like *to have been walking* in the Lake District at this time of the year.
3. I watched the ship *sink* below the waves.
4. *To have come* first in the race would have been a great honour.
5. I should like *to see* him *cycle* all that distance.

State what **function** the infinitives fulfil in these sentences:

1. *To argue* with him is a waste of time.
2. He was going round *to punch* him on the nose.
3. Can you give me a towel *to dry* myself with, please.
4. The man was about *to throw* himself off the bridge.
5. *To sit* and *doze* is my way of spending a day off.
6. The idea is *to taste* it first, not *to swallow* it whole.
7. *To jump* in the bath without stopping *to test* the temperature first is *to ask* for trouble.
8. He stopped running *to listen* if anyone was following him.

Imperative mood

This is the mood of **command** or **advice**. It occurs only in the **present tense**, and is expressed by using the 2nd person form of the verb (singular or plural), without a subject. E.g.

Go outside	('You' go . . .)
Come here at once	('You' come . . .)
Give me that book	('You' give . . .)
Dress me nicely	('You' dress . . .)

Notice that the imperative form of the verb can take an **object** ('me', 'book') and be modified by an **adverb** ('outside', 'here', 'at once', 'nicely').

A form of the **imperative mood** occurs in the 1st and 3rd persons by using the verb 'to let'. E.g.

Let me **speak** to him.
Let us **go** home now.
Let him **drive** the car.
Let them **drink** the tea.

It might, however, be simpler to regard all these examples as imperatives of the 2nd person – i.e. 'you let . . .' – and the verbs underlined as infinitives without the 'to' prefix.

The sentences would then parse thus:

Let : imperative, 2nd person, subject 'you' understood
me : indirect object of 'let'.
go : infinitive, direct object of 'let'.
home : adverb of place.
now : adverb of time.

In the negative, the imperative requires the use of the auxiliary verb 'do':

Do not **speak** to him (subject still is 'you').
Do not **touch** that exhibit.

Subjunctive mood

In modern English usage, the **subjunctive** is virtually dead.

It has been described as expressing a purpose, a wish, a doubt rather than a fact, but this description is a relic of the strong Latin influence that dominated grammatical practice for so long.

In old grammar books, parts of the verb which were formed with 'may', 'shall', 'should', 'might' and 'lest'

were regarded as being in the **subjunctive** mood. Here
it is suggested that in all such cases the mood effect is
brought about by the use of auxiliary verbs, as
explained in that section (p. 97).

Here we offer two main instances of the subjunctive
in contemporary usage that appear to be relevant:

1. Left-overs from the past.
2. In conditionals.

Left-overs: 'I shall be eighteen *come* Sunday.'
            'I wish it *were* all over.'
            'Though he *be* safe . . .?

In addition to some of these survivors from the past,
there are lines of poetry where the subjunctive still
lives:

The chariest made is prodigal enough
If she *unmask* her beauty to the moon.

If music *be* the food of love . . .

So *be it* when I shall grow old,
   Or let me die . . .

Before it *cloud*, Christ, lord, and *sour* with
   sinning . . .

Conditionals

The sensible attitude with conditional clauses is to use
the subjunctive form of the verb where the statement
is not in accordance with fact. E.g.

If I *were* innocent, I should not be worried. (But I
   am not innocent.)

If he *were* Rockefeller, he would not be driving an old banger! (But he is not Rockefeller.)

These are the only instances of subjunctive which need exercise today's student, but it must be borne in mind that other European languages may require a more rigorous attention to the implications of the subjunctive.

PARTICIPLES AND GERUNDS

In attempting to show the main functions of **participles** and **gerunds**, it will be necessary to simplify one of the minefields of English grammar. These general guidelines, however, should serve most purposes.

1. Both **participles** and **gerunds** are forms of the verb ending in -ing.
2. Participles function as **adjectives**.
3. Gerunds as **nouns**. (They are sometimes called verbal nouns.)

We shall consider them separately.

What we need to know about **participles**

1. What **kind** is it?
2. What is its **function** in the sentence?

Kinds of participles

	Active	Passive
Present:	loving	being loved

Past: –   loved
Perfect: having loved   having been loved

Note 1: Not all verbs have all these forms.
Note 2: There is no future participle in English. If needed, the future can be expressed either:

(a) by using an infinitive:

   In the days **to come**, or

(b) by the use of the preposition 'about':

   He was **about to build** a shed.

Functions of participles

1. As parts of a verbal entity:

   I am *walking*. You *have followed* him.

   This use has already been met in the conjugation of verbs and needs no further comment here.

2. Use as adjectives

   Participles can be used as descriptive adjectives:
   A **working** model, a **scheming** villain, a **shining** example, a **bleeding** wound, a **coloured** diagram, a **shattered** glass.

Notice also the detached use of the participle as an adjective:

Walking to work, the man was knocked down (describes 'man').
Singing in her bath, Mary did not hear the bell.

Reaching my house, I took out my keys.

Examples with the perfect participle:

Having baked the cake, Mother had a rest.
Having been punished, Charlie decided not to do
 it again.
Having eaten his sweets, Jim had none left to share
 with his sister.

Note 1: It is very important to ensure that the
participle relates to the subject of the sentence.
 Consider these examples:
 '*Having sat down*, the chair gave way under
him.' This is obvious nonsense. It is not the 'chair'
that has sat down!
 Similarly, '*Lying on the ground*, the aeroplane
seemed lost in the clouds to Henry.' Again, it
cannot be the aeroplane that lies on the ground.

Note 2: Although participles are used as adjectives,
they retain some of their verbal powers, and can
still take a direct object or indirect object.

 Studying maths every night, Mr Jenkins success-
 fully passed his examination.

Here 'studying' is a present participle and, as an
adjective, it qualifies the proper noun, 'Mr Jenkins'.
But it also has a direct object, 'maths', which is in
the accusative case, and is modified by the
adverbial phrase (of time) 'every night'.

 He spends his time **collecting** stamps.

'Collecting', a present participle, is an adjective
qualifying 'He' and having 'stamps' as its direct
object.

Summary of the participle

Kinds

1. Present (active)   – telling

2. Present (passive) – being told

3. Past (passive)   – told

4. Perfect (active)   – having told

5. Perfect (passive) – having been told

Function

Used as an adjective:

1. Which noun or pronoun does it qualify?

2. Does it have an object, direct or indirect?

GERUNDS (verbal nouns)

A **gerund** is part of a verb, ending in -ing, which functions as a noun, but can retain some of the characteristics of a verb.

Examples of gerunds:

I like **sleeping** (noun, from verb 'to sleep', acc. case, object of 'like').

They were accused of **breaking** and **entering** (nouns, acc. case, governed by prep. 'of').

Looting will be punished by death (nom. case, subject of 'will be punished').

Being married can be a wonderful experience. (nom. case, subject of 'can be').

Gerund with object

Drinking coffee can keep you awake (nom. case,

subject of 'can keep' and with direct object 'coffee' in acc. case).

I cannot stop him from **telling** lies (acc. case, governed by prep. 'from', and with direct object 'lies' in acc. case).

Note: As the gerund is a noun, make certain it is related as a noun to other words in the sentence.

Consider this sentence:

I did not like the girl **walking** home by herself.

'Walking' in this sentence is a **gerund**, a noun. Its case is accusative, it is the object of 'like'. What do I like? I like 'walking'. But 'walking' *belongs to* the girl. It is *her* walking we are referring to. The word 'girl' therefore must show that possession and the sentence is correctly written:

I did not like the girl's walking home by herself.

Similarly:

The *boy's* **crying** was upsetting to listen to.
The policeman thought the *man's* **driving** was erratic.
Father did not approve of *my* **going** out alone.
Aunt Ethel said she would pay for *our* **hiring** a boat for the holiday.

Occasionally these constructions can be clumsy, then the sentence has to be re-written. E.g.

She thought that Mr Smith's **insisting** on ordering more dessert was uncalled for.

This sentence can be re-written as:

She thought that Mr Smith should not have insisted on ordering more dessert.

> ### Summary of the gerund
>
> 1. What case is it in? Nominative or accusative?
> 2. Does it have an object or indirect object of its own?

Exercises on participles and gerunds

State whether the words in italics in these sentences are **participles** or **gerunds**:

1. *Walking* across the hills is good for your health.
2. I watched the cows *chewing* the cud.
3. John's *playing* football was not up to standard.
4. There were twenty people all *talking* at the same time.
5. *Whistling* for my dog, I heard no response.
6. *Thinking* of his debts drove the man to despair.
7. The *swinging* pendulum seemed to fascinate him.
8. He thought the athlete's *hurdling* would break the world record.
9. *Picking* flowers is no occupation for a man.
10. *Watching* the clock go round, Mary felt the time to stop work would never arrive.

State whether any of the words in italics have direct or indirect objects of their own.

STRONG AND WEAK VERBS

English has its roots in both the Greek/Latin and Germanic families of language. The 'strong/weak' features of a verb occur only where it is derived from Germanic sources. They affect the way the verb forms its past tense and past participle.

Weak verbs

1. Verbs which form their past tense in -d or -t when the present tense form does not end in these letters:

like, liked	push, pushed	bake, baked
pull, pulled	bang, banged	hop, hopped

2. If a verb forms its past tense by *shortening a vowel* it is termed **weak**:

feed, fed	shoot, shot	say, said

3. Where the past tense is the *same as the present tense*, verbs are said to be **weak**:

put, put	cut, cut	bit, bit

Some particular weak verbs to watch

Present tense	Past tense	Past participle
creep	crept	crept
sleep	slept	slept
keep	kept	kept

and similarly: sweep (swept), weep (wept), burn (burnt), deal (dealt), feel (felt), kneel (knelt), smell (smelt), mean (meant), spill (spilt).

Note: dream	dreamt (dreamed)	dreamt (dreamed)
lean	leant (leaned)	leant (leaned)
bring	brought	brought

and similarly: catch (caught), seek (sought), teach (taught), think (thought), sell (sold), tell (told).

then:	burst	burst	burst
	cost	cost	cost

and similarly: cut, hit, hurt, let, put, set, shut, split

but note:

	quit	quit	quit
		(quitted)	(quitted)
	knit	knit	knit
		(knitted)	(knitted)

then:	bend	bent	bent
	build	built	built
	lend	lent	lent
	send	sent	sent
	spend	spent	spent

and:	bleed	bled	bled
	breed	bred	bred

and similarly: feed, speed, meet, lead, shoot (shot).

Strong verbs

Where there is a change of vowel and no final -d or -t:

speak	spoke	spoken
sit	sat	sat
drink	drank	drunk

Note: Care has to be taken with a number of verbs about the form of the past participle.

Examples of strong verbs:

bite	bit	bitten
bind	bound	bound
blow	blew	blown
choose	chose	chosen
drive	drove	driven
fall	fell	fallen
fly	flew	flown
give	gave	given
hold	held	held
know	knew	known
ride	rode	ridden
see	saw	seen
shake	shook	shaken
sink	sank	sunk (sunken)
slay	slew	slain
steal	stole	stolen
strike	struck	stricken (struck)
swear	swore	sworn
take	took	taken
tear	tore	torn
throw	threw	thrown
tread	trod	trodden
wear	wore	worn
weave	wove	woven
write	wrote	written

Note also:

begin	began	begun
sing	sang	sung
swim	swam	swum
swing	swang	swung
run	ran	run
cling	clung	clung
fling	flung	flung
wring	wrung	wrung

dig	dug	dug
find	found	found
shine	shone	shone
sit	sat	sat
stand	stood	stood
stick	stuck	stuck
win	won	won
wind	wound	wound

There is also a category of **mixed verbs:**

beat	beat	beaten
climb	climbed	climbed
melt	melted	melted (molten)
prove	proved	proved (proven)
rot	rotted	rotted (rotten)

THE VERB 'TO BE'

The verb 'to be' can stand on its own feet as a verb, in the sense of 'to exist'. 'I am' means something, but not very much. The verb has meaning, however, in statements such as 'I am a policeman', 'I am happy'. In this way, the verb is being used in the sense of 'I exist as . . .'

A principal use of the verb 'to be', however, is as an auxiliary verb, helping to form compound tenses for other verbs. It is used to form the continuous tenses of verbs in the **active voice**, and all the tenses of the **passive voice**. Examples of the first use are:

I **am** going, he **is** swimming, we **were** driving, they **are** thinking.

Conjugation of the verb 'to be'

(The verb 'to be' is conjugated in the **active** voice only. There is no **passive** form.)

Present	*Pres. continuous*
I am	I am being
You are	You are being
He/she/it is	He is being
We are	We are being
You are	You are being
They are	They are being

Past	*Past continuous*
I was	I was being
You were	You were being
He was	He was being
We were	We were being
You were	You were being
They were	They were being

Perfect	*Pluperfect*
I have been	I had been
You have been	You had been
He/she/it has been	He had been
We have been	We had been
You have been	You had been
They have been	They had been

Future	*Future perfect*
I shall be	I shall have been
You will be	You will have been
He will be	He will have been
We shall be	We shall have been
You will be	You will have been
They will be	They will have been

Conditional	Past conditional
I should be	I should have been
You would be	You would have been
He/she/it would be	He would have been
We should be	We should have been
You would be	You would have been
They would be	They would have been

The complement

When the verb 'to be' is used as a main verb, it normally requires a **complement**.

Verb	Complement
I am	a **sailor** ('sailor' is the complement of 'I').
You are	the **man** I saw yesterday ('you' and 'man').
We have been	great **climbers** in our day ('we' and 'climber').
My **uncle** was	a **fireman** in the war ('uncle' and 'fireman').
Mary had been	a **fairy** in the play ('Mary' and 'fairy').

Note: Because, in grammar, the complement is an equivalent to the subject of the verb, it has the same case and number as the subject word.

THE VERB 'TO HAVE'

In the same way as the verb 'to be', the verb 'to have' can be used as a main verb or as an auxiliary. As a main verb it conveys a sense of possession:

John **has** a bicycle.

You **have** five minutes to get ready.
We **are having** banana sandwiches for tea.

In the sentences above, the verbs convey this sense of possession and are being used as main verbs in their own right.

The verb 'to have', however, is widely used as an auxiliary verb, part of a whole verbal idea, helping to construct the perfect tense forms of other verbs. E.g.

I **have swum** the Channel.

In this sentence, 'have swum' is the perfect tense of 'to swim'. It is regarded as one verb, although it consists of two words. (In some foreign languages it is one word.)

The guns **have been loaded** ready for firing.

The verb used here is 'to load'; 'have' and 'been' are used as auxiliaries to form what is called the passive past tense to express the exact idea of time.

Note: 'To be' and 'to have' are so widely used in the English language to form compound verbs that it is important to search out the full verb in each sentence, remembering that this verb may consist of up to four separate words:

By 1993 I **shall have been saving** my money for eight years (verb 'to save').
You **had been running** for six hours (verb 'to run').
We **should have been living** in Spain by now (verb 'to live').

AUXILIARY VERBS

The English language makes frequent use of **auxiliary verbs.** As already indicated in the sections on the verbs 'to be' and 'to have' (pp. 93 and 95), auxiliary verbs serve a twofold purpose in grammatical structures. They have a meaning of their own and can be used as principal verbs in their own right. They also combine with other verbs to form a whole verbal idea, offering subtle nuances of meaning.

These are the auxiliary verbs:

To be
To have
Can
May
Ought
Used to
Do

'Can' and 'could'

'Can' (present) and 'could' (past) are used as auxiliaries in the following ways:

Ability or fitness to perform a task:

I **can jump** six feet two.
I **can** easily **fight** him.

(*Note*: The complete verbal ideas in these sentences are 'can jump' and 'can fight').

To seek permission to do something:

Can I **have** a new book?
Can we **go** out tonight?

To show possibility or likelihood:

>My father says I **can go** with you.
>I think I **can pay** for my lunch.

'May' and 'might'

These are used in the following ways:

To indicate permission, either granted or sought:

>You and Helen **may go** to the park.
>Do you think we **might borrow** the car?

To express a possibility:

>The rope **might break**.
>You **may find** that bread indigestible.
>She may have told me.

Expressing a strong wish:

>Long **may** the Queen **reign**.
>Oh that he **might come** and rescue me!

To show courtesy:

>Whose little dog **might** you **be**?
>**May** I **borrow** some sugar?

To indicate reproach:

>She **might** have told me (but she did not).
>He **might** have come earlier (but he chose not to).

'May' and 'might' are used for emphasis, but 'might' suggests that one is less certain of the outcome.

Note: 'May' and 'can'

When permission is the issue, it is better English usage to use 'may': 'Yes, he *may do* it' rather than 'Yes, he *can do* it'.

'Ought'

Used to show duty or obligation:

> You **ought to pay** your bills.
> He **ought to go** home to his wife.

To indicate prudence in a course of action:

> You **ought to watch** your step.
> They **ought to be** more careful.

To show expectation:

> We **ought to finish** by six o'clock.
> He **ought to arrive** soon.

'Used to'

'Used to' can be employed as an auxiliary in the sense of 'having been accustomed to', or 'in the habit of doing something'.

> I **used to enjoy** walking when I was a young man.
> He **used not to come** home so late.

Avoid: 'You didn't use to wear a hat.'
write instead: 'You used not to wear a hat.'

'To do'

'Do' can be used as a principal verb with meanings of

its own, in the sense of 'to perform':

> I **did** a painting for them.
> I **have done** well in my exams.

In the sense of 'arranging something':

> **Will** you **do** my hair for me?
> I **shall do** the necessary for the party.

In the sense of 'to manage':

> How **are** you **doing** these days?
> **Are** you **doing** all right?

It is also used as an auxiliary with other verbs:

In an interrogative sentence:

> **Do** you **like** him?
> **Did** you **go** out last night?

In negative statements:

> He **does** not **swim** very far.
> They **did** not **bring** me a present.

To replace a verb already used once, to avoid repetition:

> He **went** out and **did** not come back.
> She **walked** home, and the others **did** the same.

Important: When auxiliary verbs are used, the verbal idea in a sentence will consist of **more than one word**, sometimes separated by others.

Complement and apposition

A **complement** is a word, or group of words, that completes the meaning of a statement.
Consider these sentences:

1. This book is *a first edition*.
2. I made *my nephew my heir*.
3. Mr John Brown was *the Clerk of the Court*.
4. The sailors were *castaways* on the island.

If you consider the opening words of these sentences:

1. This book is . . .
2. I made . . .
3. Mr John Brown was . . .
4. The sailors were . . .

you can see that none of them is complete as it stands.
Each phrase needs some more words to complete the
meaning. It needs a **complement**, such as the words
in italics above.

In such sentences the **complement** has the same
'case' as the original noun. *Edition, nephew* (and *heir*),
Clerk of the Court and *castaways* are all nominative
case, as are their respective counterparts: 'book', 'I',
'Mr John Brown' and 'sailors'.

Apposition

Words are said to be in apposition when their function
in a sentence is identical and when they are inter-
changeable in meaning. For example:

John, my brother, loves fishing.

'John' and 'my brother' are identical, the words denote the same person. They are in apposition.
Consider these sentences:

1. Henry Bailey, the **caretaker**, was late for work.
2. I gave my sister, **Mary**, some of my sweets.
3. Gambling, a terrible **weakness**, was his undoing.
4. She borrowed my newspaper, **The Daily Whopper**.
5. The postman handed me a parcel, a **book**.
6. The baby swallowed a sweet, a **mint humbug**.

It will be seen that the words in bold relate back to the **nouns** immediately preceding them:

Henry Bailey – **caretaker**
my sister   – **Mary**
Gambling   – **weakness**
newspaper   – **The Daily Whopper**
sweet   – **mint humbug**

The words in bold are said to be in **apposition** to the nouns in the first column and have the same case as they do (here, they are all nominative, subjects).
Words can also be in apposition to **pronouns**, e.g:

The government appointed him **Prime Minister**. ('him')
I, **John Hawkins**, am the hero of Treasure Island. ('I')
'Are you **Jane Parsons**?' the man asked. ('you')

Summary of parsing

To **parse** a part of speech we need to know a number of facts about that word's **function** in its sentence.
Here is a summary of the information we need.

Nouns
1. Kind   Proper, Common, Collective, Abstract.
2. Gender   Masculine, Feminine, Common, Neuter.
3. Case   Nominative, Accusative, Genitive.
4. Function   Subject of verb (nominative).
                 Direct object of verb (accusative).
                 Indirect object of verb (accusative).
                 Governed by preposition (accusative).
                 Showing possession (genitive).
                 Used as complement.
                 Used in apposition.

Pronouns
1. Kind   Personal, Demonstrative, Relative, Interrogative.
2. Person   1st, 2nd, 3rd.
3. Gender   Masculine, Feminine, Common, Neuter.
4. Number   Singular, Plural.
5. Case   Nominative, Accusative, Genitive.
6. Function   Subject of verb (nominative).
                 Direct object of verb (accusative).
                 Indirect object of verb (accusative).
                 Governed by preposition (accusative).
                 Showing possession (genitive).
                 With relative pronouns – antecedents should be identified.

Adjectives

1. Kind	Descriptive, Possessive, Proper, Quantitative, Numeral, Demonstrative, Interrogative, Distributive.
2. Degree	Positive, Comparative, Superlative.
3. Function	What noun or phrase does it qualify?

Adverbs

1. Kind	Time, Place, Manner, Number, Degree, Reason, Condition, Concession, Affirmation, Negation.
2. Degree	Positive, Comparative, Superlative.
3. Function	What verb, adjective or other adverb does it modify?

Verbs – Finite or non-finite?

If finite

1. Kind	Transitive, Intransitive, Auxiliary.
2. Voice	Active, Passive.
3. Person	1st, 2nd, 3rd.
4. Number	Singular, Plural.
5. Tense	Past perfect, past perfect continuous, Perfect, Perfect continuous, Past, Past continuous, Present, Present continuous, Future, Future continuous Future perfect, Future perfect continuous, Conditional, Past conditional.
6. Mood	Indicative, Imperative, Subjunctive.

If non-finite

1. Kind	Infinitive, Participle, Gerund.
2. Function	As noun equivalent. Used adjectivally. If non-finite verb has an object, this must be stated.

Verbs can also be identified as Strong or Weak.

Prepositions
1. Function   Which noun or pronoun does it govern in the accusative case?

Conjunctions
1. Kind   Co-ordinating, Subordinating.
2. Function   Words or clauses which are joined.

Interjections
Identified only.

Examples of parsing

Nouns

London dominates the south-east **corner** of **England**

'London'   – Proper noun, neuter, singular, nominative case, subject of 'dominates'.
'corner'   – Common noun, neuter, singular, accusative case, direct object of 'dominates'.
'England'   Proper noun, neuter, singular, accusative case, governed by preposition 'of'.

Lions and **lionesses** are feared by many **groups** of **animals** in **Africa** because of their **strength** and **ferocity.**

'Lions'   – Common noun, masculine, plural, nominative case, subject of 'are feared'.
'lionesses'   – Common noun, feminine, plural, nominative case, subject of 'are feared'.
'groups'   – Collective noun, common gender, plural, accusative case, governed by preposition 'by'.

'animals'   – Common noun, common gender, plural, accusative case, governed by preposition 'of'.

'Africa'   – Proper noun, neuter, singular, accusative case, governed by preposition 'in'.

'strength'   – Abstract noun, neuter, singular, accusative case, governed by preposition 'because of'.

'ferocity'   – Abstract noun, singular, neuter, accusative case, governed by preposition 'because of'.

Guided by the **usherettes**, the **audience** left the **cinema** in orderly **fashion**.

'usherettes' – Common noun, feminine, plural, accusative case, governed by preposition 'by'

'audience'   – Collective noun, common gender, singular, nominative case, subject of 'left'.

'cinema'   – Common noun, neuter, singular, accusative case, direct object of 'left'.

'fashion'   – Common (abstract?) noun, neuter, singular, accusative case, governed by preposition 'in'.

Pronouns

Will **you** give **me** that book, please. **I** did pay for **it**, **you** know. **It** was **one** of **three that I** bought for **all** of **us**.

'you'   – Personal pronoun, common gender, singular, 2nd person, nominative case, subject of 'will give'.

'me'   – Personal pronoun, common gender, singular, 1st person, accusative case, indirect object of 'will give'.

'I'   – Personal pronoun, common gender, singular, 1st person, nominative case, subject of 'did pay'.

'it'   – Personal pronoun, neuter, singular, 3rd person, accusative case, governed by preposition 'for'.

'you'   – Personal pronoun, common gender, singular, 2nd person, nominative case, subject of 'know'.

'It'   – Personal pronoun, neuter, singular, 3rd person, nominative case, subject of 'was'.

'one'   – Demonstrative pronoun, neuter, singular, 3rd person, nominative case, complement to 'it'.

'three'   – Numeral pronoun, neuter, plural, accusative case, governed by preposition 'of'.

'that'   – Relative pronoun, neuter, plural, accusative case, direct object of 'bought', refers to antecedent 'three', i.e. 'three books'.

'I'   – Personal pronoun, singular, 1st person, nominative case, subject of 'bought'.

'all'   – Demonstrative pronoun, common gender, plural, accusative case, governed by preposition 'for'.

'us'   – Personal pronoun, common gender, plural, 1st person, accusative case, governed by preposition 'of'.

The shoes were **theirs**, and **we** hope **they**'ll clean **them**.

'theirs'   – Personal pronoun, common gender, plural, 3rd person, genitive case.

'we'   – Personal pronoun, common gender, plural, 1st person, nominative case, subject of 'hope'.

'they'   – Personal pronoun, common gender, plural, 3rd person, nominative case, subject of 'will clean'.

'them'   – Personal pronoun, neuter, plural, 3rd person, accusative case, direct object of 'will clean'.

Note: All pronouns in 'common gender' can be either masculine or feminine, if the context is known.

Adjectives

My French teacher has **the bluest** eyes and **a lovely** smile.

'My'   – Possessive adj., qualifying 'teacher'.
'French'   – Proper adj., qualifying 'teacher'.
'bluest'   – Descriptive adj., superlative degree, qualifying 'eyes'.
'the'   – Definite article.
'a'   – Indefinite article.
'lovely'   – Descriptive adj., qualifying 'smile'.

Six men piled into **that old** car and caused **some** havoc in **that quietest** of streets.

'six'   – Numeral adj., qualifying 'men'.
'that'   – Demonstrative adj., qualifying 'car'.
'old'   – Descriptive adj., qualifying 'car'.
'some'   – Quantitative adj., qualifying 'havoc'.
'that'   – Demonstrative adj., qualifying 'street' (understood).
'quietest'   – Descriptive adj., superlative degree, qualifying 'street' (understood).

The taller man had **a certain** charm and I was **sure** he was **the** object of **every** person's **closest** scrutiny.

'The'	– Definite article.
'taller'	– Descriptive adj., comparative degree, qualifying 'man'.
'a'	– Indefinite article.
'certain'	– Descriptive adj., qualifying 'charm'.
'sure'	– Descriptive adj., qualifying 'I', predicatively.
'the'	– Definite article.
'every'	– Distributive adj., qualifying 'person'.
'closest'	– Descriptive adj., superlative degree, qualifying 'scrutiny'.

Which pyjamas are you wearing, **sleepy** head? The **thinner** ones, or **those nice warm** ones?

'Which'	– Interrogative adj., qualifying 'pyjamas'.
'sleepy'	– Descriptive adj., qualifying 'head'.
'thinner'	– Descriptive adj., comparative degree, qualifying 'ones' (pronoun).
'those'	– Demonstrative adj., qualifying 'ones'.
'warm'	– Descriptive adj., qualifying 'ones'.
'nice'	– Descriptive adj., qualifying 'ones'.

Adverbs

He came **home yesterday**.

'home'	– Adv. of place, modifying 'came'.
'yesterday'	– Adv. of time, modifying 'came'.

She laughed **gaily when** John fell **down twice** on the same spot.

'gaily'	– Adv. of manner, modifying 'laughed'.
'down'	– Adv. of place, modifying 'fell'.
'twice'	– Adv. of number, modifying 'fell'.
'when'	– This is an 'adverbial conjunction', com-

bining the functions of both adverb
(time) and conjunction (subordination).

Why did you go **there so often**?

'Why'	— Adv. of reason, modifying 'did go'.
'there'	— Adv. of place, modifying 'did go'.
'so'	— Adv. of degree, modifying the adverb 'often'.
'often'	— Adv. of time, modifying 'did go'.

The **awfully** handsome Captain Somers? **Yes**, I
admire him **very much**. He's fought **more bravely**
than anyone I've **ever** known.

'awfully'	— Adv. of manner, modifying the adj. 'handsome'.
'Yes'	— Adv. of affirmation.
'very'	— Adv. of degree, modifying adv. 'much'.
'much'	— Adv. of degree, modifying 'admire'.
'more bravely'	— Adv. of manner, comparative degree, modifying 'fought'.
'ever'	— Adv. of time, modifying 'have known'.

Verbs

He **had come** home before I **could get ready to go**
out.

'had come'	— Finite verb, intransitive, from vb. 'to come', active voice, indicative mood, 3rd person singular, past perfect tense.
'could get ready'	— Finite verb, intransitive, from vb. 'to get ready', active voice, indicative mood, 1st person sing-

ular, past tense, conjugated with
auxiliary vb. 'could'*

'to go'   – Infinitive, used in adverbial sense
                          of reason: why I should get ready.

                          * The verbal sense here is 'could
                          get ready', not just 'could'. For
                          this reason, the auxiliary is joined
                          with the infinitive part to form
                          one verb.

I **shall be going** early tomorrow, so **don't forget to
set** the alarm.

'shall be going'   – Finite verb, intransitive, from vb.
                          'to go', active voice, indicative
                          mood, 1st person singular, future
                          continuous tense.

'don't forget'**   – Finite verb, transitive, from vb.
                          'to forget', active voice, impera-
                          tive mood, 2nd person singular,
                          present tense.

'to set'   – Present infinitive, used as a noun,
                          direct object of 'don't forget', with
                          its own direct object, 'the alarm'.

** The actual verb is, of course, 'do forget'.

Stop that man! He **has stolen** my watch.

'Stop!'   – Finite verb, transitive, from vb.
                          'to stop', active voice, imperative
                          mood, 2nd person singular/
                          plural, present tense.

'has stolen'   – Finite verb, transitive, from vb.
                          'to steal', active voice, indicative
                          mood, 3rd person singular, per-
                          fect tense.

The girl **will be rewarded** for **preventing** the horse from **running away.**

'will be rewarded'	– Finite verb, transitive, from vb. 'to reward', passive voice, indicative mood, 3rd person singular, future tense.
'preventing'	– Non-finite, present participle, used as a noun, governed by preposition 'for', with its own direct object, 'the horse'.
'running away'	– Non-finite, present participle, used as a noun, governed by preposition 'from'.

Three boys **chose to play** football and six **thought** they **would prefer to watch** T.V.

'chose'	– Finite verb, transitive, from vb. 'to choose', active voice, indicative mood, 3rd person plural, past tense.
'to play'	– Present infinitive, used as a noun, direct object of vb. 'chose', with its own direct object, 'football'.
'thought'	– Finite verb, transitive, from vb. 'to think', active voice, indicative mood, 3rd person plural, past tense.
'would prefer'	– Finite verb, transitive, from vb. 'to prefer', active voice, indicative mood, 3rd person plural, conditional tense.
'to watch'	– Present infinitive, used as a noun, direct object of 'would prefer', with its own direct object, 'T.V.'.

Sailing is a favourite pastime of those who **have been brought up** by the sea.

'Sailing'	– Non-finite verb, a gerund, used as a noun, subject of 'is'.
'is'	– Finite verb, intransitive, from vb. 'to be', active voice, indicative mood, 3rd person singular, present tense.
'have been brought up'	– Finite verb, intransitive, from vb. 'to bring up', passive voice, indicative mood, 3rd person plural, perfect continuous tense.

Having been burnt, if I **were** you, I **would not touch** that stove.

'Having been burnt'	– Non-finite verb, past participle, used as an adjective, complement to 'I'.
'were'	– Finite verb, intransitive, from vb. 'to be', active voice, subjunctive mood, 1st person singular, present tense.
'would (not) touch'	– Finite verb, transitive, from vb. 'to touch', active voice, indicative mood, 1st person singular, conditional tense.

Prepositions

Riding **over** a bump, the boy fell **off** his cycle and landed **on** his rump.

'over'	– Preposition governing 'bump'.
'off'	– Preposition governing 'cycle'.
'on'	– Preposition governing 'rump'.

Owing to heavy rain, the trees **in** the field have been blown down.

'Owing to' – Preposition governing 'rain'.
'in'   – Preposition governing 'field'.

As an actor, Peter looked **like** a bear **with** a pair of trousers **on**.

'As'   – Preposition governing 'actor'.
'like' – Preposition governing 'bear'.
'with' – Preposition governing 'pair'.
'on'   – There is a 'rule' that sentences should not end with a preposition. This is a good rule and a bad one. In many sentences, prepositions are wrongly placed at the end and should find their way back to the nouns or pronouns they govern.

In a sentence like the one above, however, there is no other place for 'on'. Nor is the sentence a 'bad' one. What is missing, perhaps, is the sense of 'on *what* or *whom?*' Granted the omission, it is not unreasonable to 'understand' a word like 'him' to make the sense complete.

Conjunctions
These need identifying only. Mention should be made whether they are co-ordinating or subordinating conjunctions. As many of the latter are adverbial in their function, it is useful to indicate in which adverbial sense they are used.

Examples of **co-ordinating** conjunctions:

The man **and** woman went for a walk.
Neither the butter **nor** the milk was very fresh.

Father gave Jim his pocket money, **for** he deserved it.

Both Maths **and** French are my favourite subjects.

My brother could swim **but** he could not run very fast.

The bowler took five quick wickets, **and** the crowd was delighted.

Examples of **subordinating** conjunctions:

After the horse has bolted it's no use shutting the gate. (time)

Get washed **before** you go out. (time)

She would not cross the field **while** the bull was loose. (time)

Wait **until** the clock strikes six. (time)

Wherever the book is, it has to be found. (place)

Tom did not know **where** he had left his wallet. (place)

Because you are late, your tea is cold. (reason)

John missed his friend **as** he had to leave early. (reason)

Since you did not turn up we went without you. (reason)

Don't stand there **as though** you were a dummy. (manner)

Lord Rothschild is richer **than** I am. (degree)

If you dawdle, you'll be late home. (condition)

The Government will not resign **unless** they are forced to. (condition)

Although Johnny is very ill, I think there is still some hope. (concession)

Examples of parsing whole sentences

'A cynic is not merely one who reads bitter lessons from the past; he is one who is prematurely disappointed in the future.' Sidney J. Harris

'A'	– Indefinite article.
'cynic'	– Common noun, common gender, singular, nominative case, subject of 'is'.
'is'	– Finite verb, intransitive, from vb. 'to be', active voice, indicative mood, 3rd person singular, present tense.
'not'	– Adverb of negation, modifying 'merely'.
'merely'	– Adverb of degree, modifying 'is'.
'one'	– Demonstrative pronoun, 3rd person singular, common gender, nominative case, complement of 'cynic'.
'who'	– Relative pronoun, 3rd person singular, common gender, nominative case, subject of 'reads', with antecedent 'one'.
'reads'	– Finite verb, transitive, from vb. 'to read', active voice, indicative mood, 3rd person singular, present tense.
'bitter'	– Descriptive adjective, qualifying 'lessons'.
'lessons'	– Common noun, neuter, plural, accusative case, direct object of 'reads'.
'from'	– Preposition governing 'past'.
'the'	– Definite article.
'past'	– Abstract noun, neuter, singular, accusative case governed by 'from'.
'he'	– Personal pronoun, 3rd person, masculine, singular, nominative case subject of 'is'.
'is'	– Finite verb, intransitive, from vb. 'to be', active voice, indicative

	mood, 3rd person singular, present tense.
'one'	– Demonstrative pronoun, 3rd person singular, masculine, nominative case complement to 'he'.
'who'	– Relative pronoun, 3rd person singular, common gender, nominative case, subject of 'is disappointed', with antecedent 'one'.
'is disappointed'	– Finite verb, intransitive, from vb. 'to disappoint', passive voice, indicative mood, 3rd person singular, present tense.
'prematurely'	– Adverb of time, modifying 'is disappointed'.
'in'	– Preposition governing 'future'.
'the'	– Definite article.
'future'	– Abstract noun, neuter, singular, accusative case governed by 'in'.

'It is stupid of modern civilisation to have given up believing in the devil when he is the only explanation of it.' Ronald Knox

'It'	– Personal pronoun, 3rd person singular, neuter, nominative case subject of 'is'.
'is'	– Finite verb, intransitive, from vb. 'to be', active voice, indicative mood, 3rd person singular, present tense.
'stupid'	– Descriptive adjective, qualifying 'it'.
'of'	– Preposition governing 'civilisation'.
'modern'	– Descriptive adjective, qualifying 'civilisation'.

'civilisation'   – Abstract noun, neuter, singular, accusative case governed by prep. 'of'.

'to have given up' – Non-finite verb, perfect participle of 'to give up', used as gerund, nominative case, complement to 'it', and with its own direct object, 'believing'.

'believing'   – Non-finite verb, gerund, accusative case, direct object of 'to have given up'.

'in'   – Preposition governing 'devil'.

'the'   – Definite article.

'devil'   – Common noun, masculine (?), singular, accusative case governed by 'in'.

'when'   – Adverbial conjunction, subordinating.

'he'   – Personal pronoun, 3rd person singular, masculine, nominative case subject of 'is'.

'is'   – Finite verb, intransitive, from vb. 'to be', active voice, indicative mood, 3rd person singular, present tense.

'the'   – Definite article.

'only'   – Demonstrative adjective, qualifying 'explanation'.

'explanation'   – Common noun, neuter, singular, nominative case, complement of 'he'.

'of'   – Preposition governing 'it'.

'it'   – Personal pronoun, 3rd person singular, neuter, accusative case, gov. by 'of'.

Analysis

Traditionally, analysis was taught as a preliminary to the study of classical languages as well as a discipline in its own right, part of old-fashioned English language teaching. Its encouragement of close attention to syntactical structures was an indispensable help to understanding texts and a genuine source of linguistic pleasure for many students.

In these days of grammatical paganism it seems unwise to foster the virtues of such exercises too strenuously, but it is educationally negligent to ignore the benefits they bring. These can be:

1. Clarification for students of logical thought. When one argues in a coherent manner or seeks to ensure accuracy or explicitness in communication, a knowledge of the rules of syntax can ensure more control over the effectiveness of what one says or writes.
2. Help in studying foreign languages where, in many instances, the demands of formal sentence structure are more exacting than in current English usage.
3. Competence in speaking and writing 'good English'. This most basic of human accomplishments is every student's responsibility and will prove, in many cases, to be a pleasure as well.

It will provide protection against media jargon and everyday solecisms and reinforce one's self-confidence in communication. This has nothing to do with pedantry, snobbery or outmoded tradition. A man's language is his dignity, an instant token of his estimate of his own worth

Knowledge of grammar, strangely enough, is a vital ingredient in a person's character and forms part of the sub-structure on which his 'pavilion of delight' is built.

The intention here is not to exhaust students with the minutiae of analysis but to introduce them to the basic concepts. The topics offered are:

Types of sentence
Types of clause
Sentence structure i.e.
    Subject
    Enlargement of Subject
    Predicate
    Verb
    Direct & Indirect Objects
    Complement
    Extension of Verb

Examples of 'full analysis' will be included, but the object of this section is less to provide exercises in formal analysis than a wish to stimulate an instinct for the rhythm and form of well-written English, as a musician listens to a symphony and relates melodies and harmonies to the discipline of the underlying form, giving a deeper logic and significance to his enjoyment.

TYPES OF SENTENCE

We need to know what **KIND** of sentence it is.
    There are three types of sentence:

1. Simple.
2. Compound.
3. Complex.

Simple sentence

This is a statement with only one finite verb. It can be short or long.

Go home! (Verb: 'go')

Even with her fine clothes, the woman in the expensive car, with a fierce-looking Alsatian sitting next to her on the rear seat, did not impress me either by her charm or by her intelligence. (Verb: 'did . . . impress')

These are **simple sentences**, as they contain only one finite verb.

Compound sentence

A **compound sentence** consists of two or more simple sentences linked by a co-ordinating conjunction, each group of words clustered around its finite verb and having the same status as the other group. E.g.

I **saw** the boy / and / he **smiled** in a cheerful way.
The train **was** late / but / no one **complained**.
Either / we **go** to the Smiths for supper / or / they **will have to come** to us.

Complex sentence

In a **complex sentence** we have one **main clause** and one or more **subordinate clauses**.

TYPES OF CLAUSE

A **main clause** is a kind of simple sentence.
A **subordinate clause** is dependent on words or ideas contained in another clause.

Consider these sentences:

1. The man spoke to the boy.
2. The train entered the station.
3. Help yourself to some cake.

Each of these is a simple sentence, communicating one idea. We can add further ideas to these sentences in a number of ways:

A **time** idea:
1. **After supper,** the man spoke to the boy.
2. The train entered the station **two hours late.**
3. **Before bed,** help yourself to some cake.

A **place** idea:
1. The man spoke to the boy **outside the school.**
2. The train entered the station **at platform 4.**
3. Help yourself to some cake **from the cupboard.**

A **manner** idea:
1. The man spoke to the boy **in a threatening manner.**
2. The train entered the station **like a thunderbolt.**
3. **Without making a mess,** help yourself to some cake.

We can do some **describing:**
1. The man **in the blue suit** spoke to the boy.
2. The train **with a golden funnel** entered the station.
3. Help yourself to some cake **with icing on top.**

We can offer a **reason:**
1. The man spoke to the boy **to warn him.**
2. The train entered the station **to collect the mail.**
3. Take some cake **to satisfy your hunger.**

All the additions we have made to the sentences above are **phrases**. None of them contains a finite verb, so the sentences remain **simple sentences**.

Let us consider other ways of expressing additional ideas to the original sentences, this time with a **clause** containing a finite verb.

Time:
1. After he **had finished** tidying the garden, the man spoke to the boy.
2. The train entered the station before the signal **turned** green.
3. When Sam **comes** in, help yourself to some cake.

Place:
1. The man spoke to the boy where the accident **happened.**
2. There, where the track **curves** sharply, the train entered the station.
3. Help yourself to some cake where the others **are** all **standing.**

Manner:
1. The man spoke to the boy as if he **was** very angry with him.
2. The train entered the station as though it **was** not **going** to stop.
3. As though you **were** the chief guest, just help yourself to some cake.

Description:
1. The man who **organised** the sponsored swim spoke to the boy.
2. The train that **had experienced** engine trouble entered the station.
3. Help yourself to some cake you who **look** like a starving orphan.

Other descriptions:
1. The man spoke to the boy who **was crying**.
2. The train entered the station that **was crowded** with passengers.
3. Help yourself to some cake that **was baked** yesterday by Mother.

Offering a reason:
1. Because he **was pleased** to see him, the man spoke to the boy.
2. Because it **had been rerouted** earlier, the train entered the station (late).
3. As you **are** very hungry, help yourself to some cake.

The additions we have made this time are different. They all contain a **finite verb.** This means that the additional words now form a **clause**, not a phrase.

If you read out the clauses, they make some sense, but it is incomplete. We now have a **main clause** and a **subordinate clause**, making a **complex sentence.**

Note: The **subordinate clause** is dependent on a word in the main clause, and it is the nature of that dependency that determines what **kind** of subordinate clause we have.

Taking some of the sentences at random:

'*The train entered the station before the signal turned green.*'

'Before the signal turned green' tells us when the train **entered** the station. Words that tell us **when** are adverbs; the clause therefore is an **adverbial clause of time**, modifying the verb 'entered'.

'*The man spoke to the boy where the accident happened.*'

'Where the accident happened' tells us **where** the man **spoke**. Words that tell us **where** are adverbs, the clause therefore is an **adverbial clause of place**, modifying the word 'spoke'.

> '*As though you were the chief guest, just help yourself to some cake.*'

'As though . . . guest' tells us how, in what way or manner, you should **help** yourself to some cake. Words that tell us **how** are adverbs, the clause therefore is an **adverbial clause of manner**, modifying the verb 'help'.

> '*The man who organised the sponsored swim spoke to the boy.*'

'Who organised . . . swim' describes, qualifies, the 'man'. It functions like an adjective, the clause therefore is an **adjectival clause** qualifying the word 'man'.

> '*As you are very hungry, help yourself to some cake.*'

'As you are very hungry' gives us a **reason** why you should help yourself to some cake. Words that indicate reason are adverbs, the clause therefore is an **adverbial clause of reason**, modifying 'help'.

Subordinate clauses can be of three kinds:

Adverbial, adjectival or **noun.**

Note 1: A subordinate clause always refers to a word (or words) in *another* clause, main or subordinate.

Note 2: Clauses must be centred on **finite verbs**. It is useful, when analysing sentences, to pick out all finite verbs first and identify the words that are associated with each one.

Consider this sentence:

> While the baby **slept,** his mother **cooked** some meat
> so that supper **would be ready** when her husband
> **came** home.

There are four finite verbs: 'slept', 'cooked', 'would be
ready', 'came'.

This means there are four clauses:

> 'while the baby slept'
> 'his mother cooked some meat'
> 'so that supper would be ready'
> 'when her husband came home'.

The first task is to identify the **main** clause. This is
the one that is not dependent on any of the others.
   It will be seen that this (the **main** clause) is:

> 'his mother cooked the meat'

Now look at the other clauses:

'While the baby slept'	– tells us **when** she cooked = **adverbial clause of time.**
'so that supper would be ready'	– tells us **why, for what reason**, she cooked = **adverbial clause of reason.**
'when her husband came home'	– tells us **when** it 'would be ready' = **adverbial clause of time.**

This is a **complex sentence**: it has a **main** clause and three **subordinate** clauses.

Examples of subordinate clauses

Adverbial

Time:
> Fred scored the last goal **just as the whistle went**. (**When** did he score?)
> **Until you save a hundred pounds**, you cannot go to France.
> I shall wait **while you put on your coat**.

Place:
> I could not see his face **where he was standing**.
> The dog started sniffing **where the intruder had entered**.

Manner:
> Doris looked at her sister **as though she had seen a ghost**.
> **As they sow**, men will reap.

Reason:
> He is hot and flustered **because he has been running**.
> **As he works so hard**, he will succeed.

Condition:
> **If you are late for the auction**, the painting will be sold.
> The policeman would have arrested the man **if he had been there on time**.

Concession:
> **Although you are very clever**, you cannot work that computer.

Mary gave Katie her sweets **though she really wanted to keep them.**

Adjectival

I saw the lady **who told me off yesterday.**

The school had a clock **which was always ten minutes slow.**

The road **which was always dangerous in the fog** was blocked by traffic.

She bought an umbrella **that never opened properly.**

I bought a pen, **which had a gold nib,** for just sixpence.

Noun

1. *As subject:*

That he has been arrested is no concern of mine. (**What** is no concern of mine?)

What he is doing with his money worries his father a great deal. (**What** worries his father?)

2. *As object:*

I do not know **how he keeps his youthful looks.** (**What** is it I do not know?)

The film star told the press **she was delighted with her new role.** (**What** did she tell the press?)

3. *After a preposition:*

From where I am standing, he looks like my brother Paul. (**From** the spot . . .)

By 'If I never come home again', he meant he was leaving for good. (**By** those words)

4. *In apposition:*

It was obvious **that Peter was drunk.** (**It** = Peter was drunk)

Because she was ill was the reason for her absence. (**Because she was ill** = the reason)

That was **where Anne found the body**. (**That** =
where Anne found the body)

Note: Clauses may interrupt each other and may
require separating:

The man who came to dinner did not go home until
midnight.

1. The man . . . did not go home until midnight =
   main.
2. who came to dinner = **adjectival**, qualifying
   'man'.

Mother put him, when he eventually arrived,
straight up to bed.

1. Mother put him . . . straight up to bed = **main**.
2. when he eventually arrived = **adverbial of time**,
   modifying 'put'.

Note: The type of clause is determined by its **function**.
The same clause, in different sentences, satisfies
different functions:

Where I am going is no concern of yours. (Noun –
subj. of 'is')
The village **where I am going** is tucked away in the
Cotswolds. (Adjectival – qualifying 'village')
They will not be able to see my face **where I am
going**. (Adverbial – modifying 'will not be able')

SENTENCE STRUCTURE

A sentence has a number of component parts, but they
are grouped under two main headings: **subject** and
predicate.

Consider this sentence:
The author, wrestling with all kinds of difficulties and feeling the need to finish the book by the weekend, worked well into the early hours of the morning.

The essential message here is 'the author worked'. The rest of the sentence simply answers questions such as:

What kind of 'author'?
How, when, where did he work?

Consider this sentence:

Laughing at the play with much pleasure, Sally suddenly knocked the expensive box of chocolates down into the stalls of the theatre.

'Sally knocked' is the central message; the remainder tells us about Sally and what she knocked and where she knocked it.

To identify the 'essential message' of a sentence, we have first to separate the clauses. Therefore:

1. Identify the finite verbs.
2. Find their subjects.
3. Attach the other words belonging to them.

Consider this sentence:

The performing monkey jumped on top of the organ, clapping his hands and chattering in funny little noises.

1. Finite verb – 'jumped'
2. Subject – 'monkey'
3. (a) Words associated with 'monkey':

'the performing'
'clapping his hands and chattering in funny little sounds'
(b) Words associated with 'jumped':
'on top of the organ'

We now have the two parts:

Subject: 'The performing monkey, clapping his hands and chattering in funny little sounds', and
Predicate: 'jumped on top of the organ'.

My father gives presents, usually books, to all his children on their birthdays.

1. Finite verb – 'gives'
2. Subject: – 'father'
3. (a) Words associated with 'gives':
       'presents' (object)
       'usually books' (object)
       'to all his children' (indirect object)
       'on their birthdays' (**when** he gives them)
   (b) Word associated with 'father':
       'my'.

Go home at once to see your cousin.

1. Finite verb – 'Go'
2. Subject: – 'you' (understood, not spoken)
3. Words associated with 'Go':
   'home' (**where?**)
   'at once' (**when?**)
   'to see your cousin' (**why?**)

The convention is to display these sentences in a framework. This enables us to see the relationships between parts of the sentence graphically.

In the case of a complex sentence, the analysis can be extended to show the relationships **between** the clauses, as well as analysis of each clause into its constituent parts.

Consider this sentence:

When they came bounding into the arena, the clowns in their brightly-coloured costumes which, although no one would have guessed, had been patched up dozens of times, were actually six old men whom the ringmaster, from where he was standing in the centre, kept prodding with his whip, to make sure they kept the crowds laughing.

1. Pick out the finite verbs.
2. Identify the subjects.
3. Write out each clause separately;
   decide which is the main clause (or clauses);
   examine how the clauses relate to each other.

1. 'came', 'would have guessed', 'had been patched up', 'were', 'was standing', 'kept prodding', 'kept'.

2. '*they* came'
   '*no one* would have guessed'
   '*which* had been patched up'
   '*the clowns* were'
   '*he* was standing'
   '*the ringmaster* kept prodding'
   '*they* kept'

3. 'the clowns in the brightly-coloured costumes . . . were actually six old men' = **main clause**
   'when they came bounding into the arena'
      =**adverbial** (time)
   'although no one would have guessed'
      = **adverbial** (concession)

'which had been patched up dozens of times'
   = **adjectival** (descriptive)
'from where he was standing in the centre'
   = **adverbial** (place)
'whom the ringmaster kept prodding with his
   whip' = **adjectival** (relative)
'to make sure they kept the crowds laughing'
   = **adverbial** (reason).

1. The full analysis of this sentence is shown
   in Table

Table 1

| Clause | Link | Subject | Enlargement of subject | Verb | Dir. object | Extension of verb | | | Adverbial extension |
						Ind. object	Complement		
'when ... arena', (**adv.** of time)	when	they		came bounding					into the arena
'although ... guessed', (**adv.** of concession)	although	no one		would have guessed					
'which ... up', (**adj.** descriptive)		which		had been patched up					

Clause	Link	Subject	Enlargement of subject	Verb	Extension of verb			Adverbial extension
					Dir. object	Ind. object	Complement	
'the clowns . . . men' (**main clause**)		clowns	the, in the brightly-coloured costumes	were			six old men	actually
'from where . . . centre' (**adv.** of place)		he		was standing				from where . . . in the centre
'whom . . . whip' (**adj.** relative)		ring master	the	kept prodding	whom			with his whip
'to make sure . . . laughing' (**adv.** of reason)		they		kept	the crowds		laughing	to make sure

Appendix: Punctuation

It is not intended to discuss here the full range of English punctuation conventions but only to explore two areas where the marks used arise directly from grammatical needs. These are certain uses of the comma and the hyphen.

COMMAS

The comma is a notorious trouble-maker. There are many instances where its use is as much a matter of taste as it is of formula and, even where rules demand stricter observance, moments of doubt and disagreement arise over its proper use. For our present purpose we shall discuss the use of the comma with subordinate clauses and phrases. A basic point to bear in mind is that, in general, subordinate clauses, although they normally contain a subject and predicate of their own, relate to a main clause as a single word: a noun, an adjective or an adverb. Phrases do the same.

Consider these sentences:

Noun: I told him **what I was going to do** ('my plan').

Adjective: The actor **whom everyone knew** played 'Hamlet' ('famous').

Adverb: The explorer travelled **where no man had been before** ('far afield').

A general clue to punctuation in this context is to ask whether the subordinate clause is an essential part of the whole statement (in which case the use of commas would be wrong), or whether it is a comment, an extra description or extension of the verbal idea (in which case commas are more or less required).

Noun clauses and phrases

There is a distinction to be made between **noun clauses** and the other subordinate clauses. The sentences above,

'The actor . . . played 'Hamlet' and
'The explorer travelled . . .'

are more or less complete sentences on their own; the adjectival and adverbial clauses associated with them just extend the ideas they contain. This is not the case with the noun clause

'I told him . . .'

It needs completion. Indeed, the purpose of a noun clause is normally to provide a subject, an object or a complement for the main verb that is essential for the meaning, and for the grammar, of the whole sentence.

We would not place a comma in the sentence

I asked John the time.

Nor should we do so where the object of the 'asking' is a clause:

I asked John **what the time was**.

Noun clauses are frequently introduced by the word 'that', and it is this word which attracts the offending comma:

On Monday I found, that he was absent (**wrong**. No comma).

We thought that, he had been fishing by the lake (**wrong**. No commas).

All the people felt that, the king had made a serious mistake (**wrong**. No comma).

The temptation to insert a comma becomes stronger where a subject is placed a considerable distance away from its verb:

The girl in the flowing yellow dress with the beautiful green shawl over her shoulders, danced across the terrace

(**wrong**. 'The girl', subject, is not to be separated from 'danced', verb, by a comma).

The famous exploits of Bader and his brave companions during their wartime flying activities with the R.A.F., are now part of the folk-lore of our history.

(**wrong**. 'Exploits', subject, and 'are', verb, cannot be separated by the offending comma).

Parenthesis

There are sentences, however, where commas (**two**, not one) are rightly used. These occur where a phrase or clause is inserted between subject and verb, or subject and complement, and is cordoned off by two commas:

I said, **seizing the microphone to make myself heard**, that no one was to leave the hall.

The inserted phrase is properly bracketed off, fore and

aft, by commas, and these do no offence to the structure of the sentence. Likewise:

> The Prime Minister argued that, **even if one allowed for differences in language and custom**, there was no excuse for such misunderstandings to arise.

Note: Extreme care must be taken that commas do not attract the word 'that' into the parenthesis area. The two sentences above show clearly that it is an essential part of the main structure. The following sentence is **wrong**:

> I told him, **that if he eats his dinner**, he can go out to play.

The structure demands: 'I told him that . . . he can go out to play', and the first comma must come **after** 'that'.

Adjectival clauses and phrases

In discussing the work of the relative pronoun (p. 15), reference was made to defining and non-defining clauses. Defining clauses constitute an essential ingredient of a statement and cannot be omitted without depriving the sentence of meaning. Non-defining clauses, though they add comment and possibly give extra information, can be omitted and still leave the sentence meaningful.

Defining clauses (**no commas**)

> The boy **who broke the test-tube** must stay behind. (Which boy?)
> The train **that ran through the red light** came off the rails. (Which train?)

The medal **that he won at Alamein** was sold at auction. (Which medal?)

Non-defining clauses (commas **can be used**)

The River Severn, **which runs through Avon**, was in full spate. (Which River Severn? Nonsense)
My favourite policeman, **who was riding his bike**, seemed tired. (Which 'favourite policeman'? Does not make sense)
The fastest horse, **which won the race**, was a chestnut-brown. (Which 'fastest horse'? Not a sensible question)

Note: These two sentences:

The wet seat, **that Mary sat on**, was bright green in colour.
The wet seat **that Mary sat on** was bright green in colour.

In the first sentence, with commas, the point is that the seat was bright green in colour. The fact that Mary sat on it is just an aside, an added comment. In the second sentence, the meaning being conveyed is that there were a number of wet seats but the one Mary sat on, that particular one, was bright green in colour.

In this way, the strict application of punctuation 'rules' gives us an extra nuance of meaning that we would otherwise lose.

Adverbial clauses and phrases

While logic and precision operate with noun and adjectival clauses, more flexibility is permissible in punctuating adverbial clauses. The ground-rule is: If an adverbial clause or phrase occurs in the middle of a sentence, commas should be used at **both** ends of the clause. E.g.

William ran, **with amazing speed**, right round the boundary wall.

The purchaser, **if he pays cash**, can have a ten per cent deduction on the cost price.

If, however, a comma is to be omitted, for whatever reason, the omitted stop must always be at the **beginning** of the clause or phrase, never at the end. Having said that, we emphasise that in many cases even one omitted comma can, to use Fowler's description, be 'slovenly'.

Here are some examples of adverbial clauses and phrases with the commas wrongly and rightly used.

1. Tell Jimmy **when he goes to bed** he must clean his teeth.
2. Tell Jimmy **when he goes to bed**, he must clean his teeth.
3. Tell Jimmy, **when he goes to bed**, he must clean his teeth.

No. 1 and no. 3 are acceptable. The comma in no. 2 has some rhetorical force but it cannot be accepted on grammatical grounds.

1. I shall warn him that **whether he likes it or not** he shall pay for the damage.
2. I shall warn him that, **whether he likes it or not** he shall pay for the damage.
3. I shall warn him that, **whether he likes it or not**, he shall pay for the damage.
4. I shall warn him that **whether he likes it or not**, he shall pay for the damage.
5. I shall warn him, that **whether he likes it or not** he shall pay for the damage.

No. 1 and no. 3 are acceptable. No. 2 and no. 5 are wrong, unacceptable. No. 4 may find favour, but it again is not justifiable from a grammatical viewpoint.

Where adverbial clauses and phrases occur at the beginning or end of a sentence, they are better served if separated by a comma from the main clause:

If it rains tomorrow, I shall not go out.
While we are away, our furniture will go into store.
He won't answer the door, **even though you bang several times.**
Tommy was spending money last night, **as though it was his last night on earth.**

But observe these:

I won't be in **when you come home.**
The car skidded **because the road was covered in ice.**
As she came in Mother dropped her shopping all over the floor.
My brother looked **as if he had seen a ghost.**

It will be instinctively felt that in these sentences commas are not needed. The shortness of the sentence and the immediacy of the adverbial relationship between subordinate and main clauses make any such stoppage unnecessary and, indeed, inadvisable.

In punctuating sentences with subordinate clauses, writers have to develop an instinct for the right thing to do, but need to bear in mind all the time the grammatical logic which provides a correct foundation on which to build.

HYPHENS

(A full account of the use of the hyphen is given by H.W. Fowler, *Modern English Usage*, 1957, pp. 243–8. Ambitious scholars should pay close attention to his advice. No attempt is made here to discuss the difficulties involved in the use of this mark with similar thoroughness. We outline some of its main uses and abuses and try to alert students to the pitfalls engineered by this deceptive operator.)

If the comma is a notorious trouble-maker, the hyphen is a master strategist working, for the most part, for the enemy. Its wrong use and wrong non-use can sabotage a writer's intentions. Consider these points:

1. Unless hyphens are necessary they should be done without.
2. There are three ways by which words can be closely linked, when meaning requires this to be done:
   (a) By placing words next to each other to convey one meaning, e.g. Home Office, kitchen sink, open air, sign language.
   No hyphen is needed to bind these words, the singleness of their meaning is clear.
   (b) Adjectives and nouns, or gerunds used as nouns, which define one idea, may require a hyphen as a link, otherwise confusion could arise, e.g. A 'walking stick' is a stick that walks. If we require a word to denote a 'stick used for walking', we have to use a hyphen, 'walking-stick'. Thus: 'a fishing-rod', 'a rocking-horse', 'a swimming-costume'.

Note: Phrases too can be used as adjectives. In such cases the words of the phrase must be hyphenated: British Steel, milk pudding, but British-Steel shares, milk-pudding basin.

Omission of the hyphen in these instances reduces the phrases to nonsense.

British Steel shares = shares made of steel which happen to be British.

milk pudding basin = a pudding basin made of milk.

(c) A third way, very common in our language, is one where as a result of close association, probably over a long period of time, two separate words have coalesced to form one, e.g. handkerchief, daybreak, lifetime, tea-spoon.

These considerations bring us some guidelines for the correct use of the hyphen. It can be used:

1. To form a single word from two or more separate words. These new words can be temporary:

   the Lord-Mayor's Fund
   the London-Underground enquiry

   (If the last combination seems strange, think what the words mean without the hyphen.)

   Or they can be permanent:

   a stick-in-the-mud, half-Nelson,
   a landing-stage.

2. It can also be used to combine two adjectives to form a compound adjective:

   red-hot, hard-bitten, like-minded, new-born.

3. Adverbs and prepositions which are not normally hyphenated to their parent verbs acquire a hyphen when used as part of a participle:

'I put him up to it', but 'It was a put-up job'
'The ship came in to the harbour' but 'The in-
coming ship . . .'
'She went out to the theatre' but 'She was an
out-going . . .'

In general

A rigorous examination of the exact meaning that a compound idea is meant to convey will help to ensure correct use of the hyphen.

Words are linked by a hyphen when the oneness of the combination demands it but does not require them to be amalgamated into one word.

Here are some examples of necessary hyphens:

sought-after, an under-achiever, a new by-law, child-centred, man-made, brother-in-law, maid-of-honour, passer-by, engine-driver, happy-go-lucky, three-legged, cold-hearted, smooth-tongued, will-o'-the-wisp, cat-of-nine-tails, rose-coloured.

These, on the other hand, are single words:

overcrowded, amidships, beforehand, downtrod-den, offside, landlady, grandfather, scatterbrained.

Watch some combinations:

hand to mouth, in no way, none the less, no one, at any rate, up to date.

But note, an up-to-date list: when used as an adjective up-to-date is hyphenated.

We conclude with a plea for logic and good sense.

1. Where a hyphen is not needed to secure the relationship between two parts of a unified idea, do not put one.

2. Where the two (or more) separate parts of an expression need closely securing together for a unity of meaning, put a hyphen between them.

3. Always check that a hyphen makes sense and does not tie words together wrongly. (A 'superfluous hair-remover' is a 'hair-remover' that no one wants!)

4. Some words have joined themselves together permanently, so do not separate them by inserting an intrusive hyphen.

A reliable dictionary should provide a check for the correct use of hyphens, but some contain arguable illustrations.

Index